Interpretive Perspectives

A Collection of Essays on Interpreting Nature and Culture

LARRY BECK | TED CABLE

interpPress

ISBN-13: 978-1-879931-27-5

NATIONAL ASSOCIATION FOR
INTERPRETATION

The National Association for Interpretation is a private nonprofit [501(c)3] organization and professional association. NAI's mission is: "Inspiring leadership and excellence to advance natural and cultural interpretation as a profession." For information, visit www.interpnet.com.

For our students—

the next generation of professionals who give us hope for the future

And to seasoned interpreters—

who have persevered and thrived in the profession and who will pass on their heart-felt convictions, commitment, and passion to our students.

Contents

Foreword

by Paul Caputo

Interpretation is a funny field. It is at once relatively new, the term itself coined within the last century by John Muir, and as old as history, sometimes laughingly called the real oldest profession. Those outside the profession frequently misunderstand it, mistaking it for something to do with language, dance, or services for the deaf. And more than in most fields, those inside the profession debate the meaning, appropriateness, and even spelling of the term—or whether the field should be called something else altogether.

Every year or so, one of the publications produced by the National Association for Interpretation (NAI) runs an article delving into the issue of whether the term interpretation is appropriate for what interpreters do. More than any other issue addressed in the pages of NAI's publications, these articles touch off a firestorm of passionate responses, each offering a unique insight into the psyche of this profession. Even this book touches on the subject in the essay "Resolving the Interpreter's Identity Problem" in Chapter 3.

A field with this much uncertainty needs voices like Larry Beck's and Ted Cable's, who make interpretation accessible to beginners and who offer inspiration to seasoned veterans. Together, they have written a textbook on interpretation (Interpretation of Cultural and Natural Resources, with Doug Knudson) and independently, they have written interpretive or informational books like Larry Beck's Moving Beyond Treeline and Ted Cable's Birds of the Great Plains and Driving Across Kansas. But in my opinion, it is their 1998 book, Interpretation for the 21st Century, that defines their place in the interpretive pantheon. The book's "Fifteen Guiding Principles for Interpreting Nature and Culture" pay homage to Freeman Tilden's six principles, now half a century old, and build on them to help interpreters meet new challenges in new times.

By the time I became NAI's art and publications director in 2002, Larry Beck and Ted Cable were household names in the profession. They had won numerous NAI awards, served as editor or on the editorial board of NAI publications, and their names appeared frequently in archives of the publications that had been placed in my care. The very first issue of the Journal of Interpretation

Research to be published after my arrival at NAI featured an essay titled "The Meaning of Interpretation," written by Larry Beck and Ted Cable. (That essay appears in Chapter 7 of this book.) I have been fortunate to have the opportunity to get to know the authors in my tenure with NAI, and to continue to work with them through their contributions to Legacy magazine and the Journal of Interpretation Research.

Unfortunately, the nature of periodical publications is that they are all too easy to discard, and while much of their content is timeless, useful, and inspirational, the physical pages are all too ephemeral. (The world may never have known Aldo Leopold's A Sand County Almanac had the author's family and friends not edited and finalized a collection of essays that Leopold wrote over the last 12 years of his life.) Interpretive Perspectives pulls articles by Larry Beck and/or Ted Cable from archives as far back as 1989 and sheds the light of a new decade on them. They have been reworked and arranged by subject matter, collected and preserved for the benefit of the field of interpretation.

Whether you are new to the field or an experienced interpreter, you will be inspired by Larry Beck and Ted Cable's unique ability to find interpretive lessons in tangential fields, beauty in the everyday, and hope in the future.

Introduction

This book consists of a series of our essays that appeared in National Association for Interpretation (NAI) publications. The articles were carefully selected from all our contributions to NAI outlets and do not represent everything we have written on our own, together, or with others in these publications. This select collection of essays is intended to offer timeless themes about the interpretive profession and how to practice interpretation. We have added new biographical essays and arranged the other articles into six broad categories.

Interpretive Perspectives begins with a personal essay by each author that touches on our dedication to the profession through our personal lives, work in the profession, and writing. Our intent here is to offer biographical reflections describing our backgrounds and how they shaped the work we have done in the broad field of interpretation. We share what attracted us to the interpretive profession in essays titled "A Passion for Wilderness" and "A Passion for Birds," respectively. We tell our stories in such a way that others might identify with our experiences. In other words, we hope to strike a resonant chord with readers who may find commonalities in how they, too, were initially inspired by some facet of heritage interpretation, and how this might be sustained over an entire career and lifetime.

The second section is titled "Voices from Literature and the Arts." We begin with an essay, "To Enjoy Understandingly," that takes into account the necessity of both learning about and enjoying our cultural and natural legacy. This first selection was inspired by an essay written by naturalist John Burroughs in 1912. The second essay, "Musings on Interpretation," offers insight into the interpretive profession by award-winning author Barry Lopez. The issues raised are pertinent to the state of interpretive practice today and into the future. The third essay, "Lee Stetson on Interpretation," offers expert counsel from a professional actor on promoting environmental messages through the arts. The profession continues to expand by utilizing the arts for effective and meaningful interpretive presentations.

The third section, "Professionalism," offers discussion of some pressing issues that relate to interpreters. The lead essay is titled "Resolving the Interpreter's Identity Problem." Since its beginnings, the field of heritage interpretation has been plagued by confusion with foreign language interpreters. We offer straightforward suggestions for minimizing the confusion. The second essay in this section, "Becoming Better Interpreters," offers suggestions on how to strive for excellence in our work and lives through reading, travel, and establishing a personal identity.

The fourth section of the book is about "Application." Here we offer two articles that are directly related and followed one another in publication: "A Pocketchange History of the Lewis and Clark Expedition" and "Interpreting Our State's Heritage." Both of these essays focus on the creative use of those obvious things that surround us daily to interpret effectively.

The fifth section, "Universal Concepts," concentrates on explaining an important—and relatively new—approach to interpretation. Promoted by the National Park Service, this approach is not fully understood by many outside of that agency. The basics of tangibles, intangibles, and universal concepts are presented first in the context of one of our National Association for Interpretation annual workshops ("What is the Essence of Our Professional Responsibility?") and next in the context of musical theater ("Wicked Interpretation: Lessons from Broadway").

The sixth section of the book is titled "Global Interpretation." We offer two articles in this category. The first essay, "The Role of Interpretation in International Tourism," reveals the importance of interpretation as an agent of peace and global conservation. The second essay explores ways in which volunteer travel may revolutionize the tourism industry ("VolunTourism: Seeing the World and Saving the World"). These essays indicate the importance of travel in promoting global environmental integrity and international peace.

The seventh and final section of the book is about "Inspiration." The first essay, "Interpretive Lighthouses," suggests that interpretation provides direction and inspiration to light the way as people strive to learn about and experience the world. Like lighthouses, our interpretive centers illuminate the hidden meanings of our surroundings and guide travelers through unfamiliar places. The second essay is titled "The Need for Interpretation: Now More Than Ever." It is a reflection on the terror attacks of September 11, 2001 and the place of interpretation in such a world. The third essay is titled "The Meaning of Interpretation: The Gift of Hope" and is followed by our conclusion, a new essay titled "A Profession of Hope." Given the many challenges we face in the world today, we close with these thoughts on having a positive, action-oriented, and hope-filled response to those challenges. Such a response comes both in our personal lives and what we offer others, through interpretation, in our professional lives.

1

Biographical Stories: The Authors

A Passion for Wilderness

Wilderness offers adventure, freedom, simplicity, beauty, inspiration, and wonder. Larry Beck describes how he was inspired to become an interpreter and then to teach about cultural and environmental interpretation through his passion for wilderness.

"In wildness is the preservation of the world." —Henry David Thoreau

Passion for the outdoors and curiosity about all things natural brought me into the profession of cultural and natural history interpretation. I was raised in southern California at a time when open space and orange groves were still the rule. As a kid I explored the native coastal sage scrub on the hills that surrounded my home. I was fascinated with all living creatures, but had a special affinity for butterflies, flashes of brilliant colors on the wing.

My parents were both educators and so we had the summers off with frequent camping trips to the beaches and mountains. One summer my parents packed the whole family into a camper and we took off to see America with stops at many of our major national parks and historic sites. I was 10 years old at the time and kept a record of all we saw in a large portfolio, complete with educational brochures from the places we visited. From an early age I had a passion for wild places and wanted to learn as much as I could about them.

In high school my favorite courses were biology and physiology. As soon as my friends and I were old enough to drive we ventured north to the mountains of the High Sierra where we camped, hiked, fished, and backpacked in the wilderness. On my first backpacking trip to the Sierras in winter, I was ill-equipped. Most of my friends had good equipment. I packed my gear into a backpack I bought for a quarter at a garage sale. The only sleeping bag I had was a cotton bag used during summer camping trips with the family. I didn't have hiking boots, so I found some old galoshes to wear over my tennis shoes. The landscape was covered with snow and it was bitter cold. I nestled close to the fire, which another friend and I kept stoked throughout the night, to have a chance at sleep. The very last night I fell asleep and actually felt warm for the first time on the trip, then discovered I had inadvertently shifted into the fire pit. I woke up with my sleeping bag on fire and rolled several times to put the flames out. I remember feeling humbled as I trudged back to the trailhead, yet also exalted by the stunning beauty that surrounded me.

In college, I started as a pre-med biology major. I soon discovered that I didn't like the laboratory courses, but really enjoyed the field courses. I piled up units in vertebrate field biology and field botany. During the summers I worked for Riverside County Parks in California, first working in park operations and then interpretation. By the time I hit my senior year at University of California–Riverside, I realized my preference was being in the field and I transferred to Humboldt State University to complete a degree in natural resource planning and interpretation.

While at Humboldt I thought it might be a good idea to backpack an inflatable raft to the Tall Trees Grove (tallest trees in the world) in the winter, then inflate my little raft and float back down Redwood Creek in flood stage…solo. I hiked the 12 miles to the Tall Trees Grove and spent the night alone among the magnificent redwoods. The next morning I inflated my raft with my lungs and set on the water as more rain began to fall. The creek was higher and faster than I'd ever seen it.

Just ahead, a huge tree had fallen into the swollen river. I rowed like crazy to avoid a collision, but it seemed the harder I rowed the more the powerful current forced me toward the tree. I hit the tree broadside and was knocked out of the raft into the swift waters. My raft was pinned on the tree by the current and my backpack had sunk into the water, although still tied to the raft.

I swam for shore and finally made it to the steep and slippery cliff. After working my way slowly back upstream I swam out into the main current to try to retrieve the raft. The first two attempts I was swept past the raft by the raging current. The third time I swam out even further and this time was properly positioned for the current to slam me directly into the tree where I held on for dear life. I was able to hoist my backpack and free the raft simultaneously, but I had lost an oar in the ordeal and the raft had a four-foot gash down the middle from the initial collision. I perched on my upside-down dinghy and paddled with one oar, mostly making circles. I finally made it back to the trailhead at dark, half-drowned and hypothermic.

My passion for wilderness went on unabated. I kept getting beat up and yet I kept coming back for more adventure, exhilaration, solitude, peace, inspiration, awe, beauty, and wonder. I was fully aware that this thing I had so much desire for could also crush me. And yet the danger only reinforced and enhanced my rapture and reverence. Years later I was on a canoe expedition in the Northwest Territories of Canada. I wrote a little book about that wilderness experience and conveyed the exuberance of voyageurs, whom I could relate to, that first explored the far north:

> The paradox of this happy life is that it revolved around hardship and danger. Voyageurs experienced the rewards of an outdoor lifestyle—a joyous state that comes from exercise, fresh air, comradeship, simplicity, and freedom. They were blessed with timeless days on the water, in full song, amidst a backdrop of exhilarating beauty. Yet this was complemented

by depravation and exposure to those same natural elements which could kill them. These seemingly contradictory forces contributed to an exuberant lifestyle that wasn't, perhaps, otherwise possible. Their highs were appreciated more since they also withstood the lows and understood the risks associated with what they were doing. They lived on the edge and would have it no other way.

Upon graduation I was able to work for the National Park Service as an interpreter at Glen Canyon. This became a hub for adventures to all sorts of national parks and monuments such as Bryce, Zion, Capitol Reef, Arches, Canyonlands, Natural Bridges, Grand Canyon, and many state parks and national forests. These years were followed by a stint with the Bureau of Land Management as a river ranger on the San Juan River in southeastern Utah. Next I returned to interpretive work with the National Park Service at Cabrillo National Monument (California) and then to Denali National Park and Preserve in Alaska.

But, as it turns out, I was also excited by the adventure of the mind. I eventually pursued graduate school and earned my Ph.D. in education from the University of Minnesota where I was also able to spend time in the Boundary Waters Canoe Area Wilderness. Then I accepted a position at San Diego State University (SDSU).

I have been at SDSU for the balance of my career, with one exception. During a budget crisis in California 15 years ago, I took a job at Kansas State University (KSU). I was only there a short time, but it was at KSU that I met Ted Cable. He showed me around the prairie landscape, pointing out birds along the way, and we discovered a shared passion for nature and interpreting the forces that make places special. This shared joy for interpretation led to a writing relationship that continues to this day.

I returned to SDSU, where I continue to teach and write about wilderness, the symbolism and meaning of protected places, and cultural and environmental interpretation. My passion for this discipline continues and I delight in sharing my experience with students.

A passion for wilderness led to working in magnificent places and interpreting those resources to others. That ultimately led to teaching and writing about wilderness and interpretation, yet another way to promote these special places and to motivate people to take advantage of the life-enriching experiences found in nature. In addition, I continue to strive to personally experience these glorious landscapes we have set aside and have made it a point to share my passion for nature and culture with my two sons and all those whom I come in contact with along my journey. Finally, I have come to vicariously experience the splendor of our parks through the experiences and joy of my students who are privileged to work at these places.

A Passion for Birds

Naturalists enter into their relationships with nature through different portals. Ted Cable describes how he was inspired to become an interpreter and then to teach about wildlife and interpretation through his passion for birds.

"Our ability to perceive quality in nature begins, as in art, with the pretty. It expands through successive stages of the beautiful to values as yet uncaptured by language."

—Aldo Leopold

This quote, routed in a piece of wood, hung over the doors of Sandridge Nature Center in a Cook County Forest Preserve, 30 miles south of downtown Chicago. When I first read it as a 21-year-old weekend naturalist, I had no idea that it would shape my professional life.

My first interpretation job (although I would not know that it was called interpretation until many years later) was as a part-time naturalist at Sandridge. I took this position because I had recently become passionate about birding and I thought I might see birds while I worked. Birds brought me into the profession.

As a young boy I had a copy of the Golden Nature Guide for birds (older readers may recall blue cover with robins on it). On family vacations I would look for those 112 birds—the only 112 birds in the world as far as I knew. But this interest waned and was non-existent during adolescence and teenage years. That changed one Saturday morning on Chicago's lakefront during my senior year in the pre-med program at the University of Illinois–Chicago. While on the weekly ornithology field trip, I saw a black-throated green warbler flitting weakly at my feet. Migrants are often fatigued after migrating over Lake Michigan, and this bird, like many migrants here, allowed exceptionally close inspection. Its beauty astounded me. This discovery, in the shadow of what was at the time the world's tallest apartment building, hooked me. On the way home, I stopped off at the Sandridge Nature Center and saw a stunning orange and black American redstart flickering like a flame. Then a male yellow warbler, an animated piece of sunshine, flew into a trailside willow and serenaded me with its "sweet sweet sweet sweeter than sweet" song. Moments later a dapper blue-gray gnatcatcher became my favorite bird—at least until this fickle novice birder saw the next new bird.

That day was a life-changing and defining moment that set the course for my entire adult life. The avian possibilities seemed endless. Feathered treasures were waiting to be discovered everywhere, even in the city. I embraced the fun and challenging sport of seeing how many species I could see on Saturday mornings in downtown Chicago. Within a few months I was leading the Saturday bird walks in Chicago's lakefront city parks. I learned that it is equally exciting to show new birds to beginning birders. Their excitement is mutual and contagious.

This new-found passion not only prompted me to take the Cook County naturalist job but birds subsequently motivated me to take my second seasonal interpretation job as a summer naturalist for Lake County Parks and Recreation in northwest Indiana.

After teaching high school science for a couple of years, birds brought me to Purdue University, where I studied marsh birds while earning a master's degree in wildlife ecology. Birds then led me to a job with Indiana's Threatened and Endangered Species State Heritage Program. I began choosing projects, meetings, and vacations based on birds.

As I traveled on birding adventures, I often was reminded that not all birds are pretty. In fact, birders called non-native and abundant birds "trash birds," "junk birds," or "dirt birds" as familiarity bred contempt. Despite this normative jaded attitude, I found it impossible to despise colorful and intelligent starlings, friendly house sparrows, and portly pigeons in the park. I adopted Walt Whitman's perspective that "a mouse is miracle" and expanded it to these "junk birds." These avian rodents were miracles too.

The Leopold quote from those early years at Sandridge Nature Center floated in my consciousness. My appreciation of nature began with the pretty—black-throated green and yellow warblers and blue-gray gnatcatchers. But it did not end with the pretty. Starlings, sparrows, and pigeons lack prettiness, but were beautiful. John Ruskin wrote, "Fitness is the first element of beauty." Starlings, pigeons, sparrows and even mice are imminently fit, thereby possessing this first element of beauty. I would learn much later that Freeman Tilden made this same point by sharing the following dialogue:

> "Can a dung basket, then," said Aristippus, "be a beautiful thing?" "Yes, by Jupiter," returned Socrates, "and a golden shield may be an ugly thing, if the one be beautifully formed for its particular uses, and the other ill formed."

Many plants, animals, and habitats that lack prettiness are beautiful because they exhibit fitness and form.

My interest in exposing people to the beauty of birds came to exceed my interest in avian biology. Although I had worked as a naturalist for two county park agencies I had never heard of interpretation. While working on my M.S. in wildlife ecology I was introduced to Doug Knudson. Doug taught me that the profession of interpretation would allow me to help people see beauty in their surroundings (not to mention to put me in a position to see beauty and birds myself). I enrolled in the Ph.D. program under Doug, and in my first interpretation course both my hall exhibit and interpretive talk focused on the turkey vulture—a beautiful bird, in function and form, that is not pretty.

George Bernard Shaw wrote, "This is the true joy of life; the being used up for a purpose recognized by yourself as a mighty one; being a force of nature instead of a feverish, selfish little clot of ailments and grievances, complaining that the world will not devote itself to making you happy." Purpose not only is a key to a joyful life, but it is linked to passion, professionalism and peace.

Interpreters must have a grand purpose to guide their work. Our 15th and final principle of interpretation, from Interpretation for the 21st Century, is the passion principle, stating, "Passion is the essential ingredient for powerful and effective interpretation." One cannot have passion without a purpose, and a strong purpose begets passion. Passion and purpose are steadfastly linked. Passion in turn leads to professionalism. Passionate interpreters desire to excel at the art of interpretation.

Finally, passionate and purposeful interpreters, striving for professionalism, experience an inner peace or contentment that comes when a person is pursuing a calling that is consistent with other priorities, beliefs, and values. As Gandhi noted, "Happiness is when what you think, what you say, and what you do are in harmony."

My professional mission statement—my professional purpose based upon the aforementioned Leopold quote—is, "To see beauty in people, plants, animals, and landscapes that are not necessarily pretty and help others do the same." It has guided virtually every aspect of my professional work.

To this end, I have authored or coauthored books to encourage people to see the beauty of birds, books to help travelers see the subtle roadside beauty of Kansas and Missouri and the beautiful acts of perseverance and resourcefulness of the people who lived along the highway, a book highlighting the beautiful dedication and courage of West African conservationists, and two interpretation books to instruct others in the art of interpreting beauty. My freelance magazine articles have attempted to provoke people to visit landscapes or closely observe species whose beauty might be overlooked. Through courses, speaking engagements, and workshops I have encouraged students and practitioners to inspire people to see the beauty of cultural resources and nature, particularly those mundane miracles that they come in contact with every day.

Interpreters are uniquely placed to enrich lives in this way. People are surrounded by beauty. With the help of interpreters they just need to stop and take in the mundane miracles—things we take for granted. By looking at an insect, flower, or bird, even a "junk bird" more closely, they become amazing things. "It is only with the heart that one can see rightly: what is essential is invisible to the eye," wrote Saint Exupery, adding, ". . . the eyes are blind. One must look with the heart." Interpreters turn hearts toward beauty.

This also applies to seeing beauty in less-than-pretty people. Although the words are seldom spoken, some people are labeled and treated as "junk" people. It has been said that true genius is looking at a "homely caterpillar, an ordinary egg, and a selfish infant, and seeing a butterfly, an eagle, and a saint." Interpreters can demonstrate this genius as they interpret peoples both past and present.

Because birds are so conspicuous, elegant, and animated, they have provided a great way to introduce and connect people with the beauty of nature. By exposing people to the beauty of birds—a ubiquitous manifestation of nature's beauty—my hope has been to get people to fall in love with birds, and through that emotional connection, to become passionate about nature in general. But my primary goal in revealing the beauty in the ordinary is not to make every person I come in contact with a naturalist, but rather to make the people I come in contact with happier people. This has been my joy, my privilege, my work, and my blessing.

"Blessed is he that has found his work. Let him ask no other blessedness." —Thomas Carlyle

2

Voices from Literature and the Arts

To Enjoy Understandingly

In the early 20th century "natural history" became a major literary genre. John Burroughs was among the best-known authors for his many articles and books. The counsel he advocates here is as pertinent today as when he wrote a century ago.

Many of us who enter into the profession of interpretation eventually end up behind desks, indoors, doing paperwork. We often tolerate this separation from nature for the sake of moving up into positions of greater responsibility and greater financial reward. These responsibilities often fail to nurture the emotional attachment to nature which initially drew us into the profession. Moreover, the scientific training that many of us have received often encourages a clinical detachment from phenomena being studied. Emotions may undermine the quality of the data or its interpretation, and yet most of us have emotional links to nature that brought us into the profession. As a result, at times, interpreters struggle with an identity issue. Are we "nature lovers" emotionally linked to nature, detached scientists studying nature, educators teaching a particular body of knowledge about nature, something in between, or all of those? Introspective interpreters may have thought about their relationship to nature as it relates to carrying out their daily job-related tasks.

John Burroughs wrote an essay titled "The Gospel of Nature" in 1912. He dealt with this same issue of identifying and articulating his relationship with nature. The following is an excerpt from this essay that has much to say about who we are as interpreters, and how we might approach our interpretation. It may even remind you of conversations you have had about your role in helping other people relate to nature.

> I am not always in sympathy with nature-study as pursued in the schools, as if this kingdom could be carried by assault. Such study is too cold, too special, too mechanical; it is likely to rub the bloom off Nature. It lacks soul and emotion; it misses the accessories of the open air and its exhilaration, the sky, the clouds, the landscape, and the currents of life that pulse everywhere....
>
> To absorb a thing is better than to learn it, and we absorb what we enjoy. We learn things at school; we absorb them in the fields and woods and on the farm. When we look upon Nature with fondness and appreciation she meets us half way and takes a deeper hold upon us than when studiously conned. Hence I say the way of knowledge of Nature is the way of love and enjoyment, and is more surely found in the open air than in the schoolroom or the laboratory....
>
> I know it is one thing to go forth as a Nature-lover, and quite another to go forth in a spirit of cold, calculating, exact science. I call myself a Nature-lover and not a scientific naturalist. All that science has to tell me is welcome, is, indeed, eagerly sought for. I must know as well as feel. I am not merely contented, like Wordsworth's poet, to enjoy what others understand. I must understand also; but above all things, I must enjoy. How much of my enjoyment springs from my knowledge I do not know. The joy of knowing is very great; the delight of picking up the threads of meaning here and there, and following them through the maze of confusing facts, I know well. When I hear the woodpecker drumming in the woods, and know what it is all for, why, that knowledge, I suppose, is part of my enjoyment. The other part is the associations that those sounds call up as voicing the arrival of spring; they are the drums that lead the joyous procession.
>
> To enjoy understandingly, that, I fancy, is the great thing to be desired.

As professionals should we identify ourselves primarily as "nature lovers" or "scientific naturalists"? We happen to agree with Burroughs that it is better to absorb a thing than to learn it. A raw, undiagnosed, fundamental connection with nature is very powerful in our lives.

Freeman Tilden's philosophy is consistent with this line of thinking. His principles state that information alone is not interpretation and that interpretation is not merely instruction. Although our official "mission" often is to provide information and spread knowledge, most of us would agree with Tilden who recognized that "people are with us mainly seeking enjoyment, not instruction." Moreover, Tilden's focus on the "priceless ingredient" (i.e., love) confirms his willingness to recognize that emotional attachments and enjoyment are a critical part of interpreting nature. More directly Tilden wrote, "Emotions are superior to facts."

Yet, as both Burroughs and Tilden point out, we must present knowledge to make our communications meaningful. And, furthermore, knowledge itself contributes to the enjoyment and "absorption" of nature. Likewise, studies have documented that even in classroom settings learning is linked to positive emotional connections to the subject matter.

So, what is the balance to strive for? We believe it is as Burroughs succinctly stated: to enjoy understandingly. That is the goal we strive for personally in our relationship with nature, and that may be a goal that other interpreters will strive for as well. More importantly, it can be a goal for our audiences—to help them enjoy understandingly. To enjoy first, but nurture and shape that joy with understanding. Our primary purpose should be to assist people in engaging with places of cultural and natural history firsthand where they might enjoy these special sites according to their own aspirations, passion, and agenda.

Then we add interpretation of the resource to enhance the experience. Among other things we can explain the natural forces that make special landscapes beautiful and meaningful. Diminishing the mystery will not take away from the sense of awe, wonder, and delight; enjoyment and knowledge can—and should—increase together.

Indeed, what good is it to merely know about nature, if you don't enjoy it? Or, as Burroughs said, "What is knowledge without enjoyment, without love?"

Musings on Interpretation

Barry Lopez is the highly acclaimed author of many books. He is the recipient of the American Book Award and the John Burroughs Medal, among other literary honors. He is among the most gifted and articulate of contemporary nature writers. Lopez was invited to participate in a lecture series titled "Promoting Environmental Messages Through the Arts" at San Diego State University where he was interviewed for this essay. Ralph Waldo Emerson wrote, "Truly speaking, it is not instruction, but provocation that I can receive from another soul." This is the gift that Lopez offers.

Barry Lopez is anguished by the contemporary American lifestyle. He has traveled extensively on several continents and has been introduced to radically different cultural points of view. In Arctic Dreams, Lopez quotes an anthropologist as saying, "You ignore at your peril the variety in human culture." Lopez is not convinced that our way of life is the best. He is not impressed with a society that is so shallow that "a bumper sticker passes for a philosophy." You sense his contempt for video games, fast food, USA Today, and Disneyland. People don't seem to have time to listen to a story, eat a lingering meal, read a real newspaper, or to stop and look and learn from nature. According to Lopez, "We live in a society in which everything has to be entertaining before it is considered valuable."

It is this mentality that presents the greatest challenge to interpreters of cultural and natural history. We are in a "terrible cul-de-sac" where even the landscape is evaluated based on its entertainment value. This "deranged illusion" holds that "nature better dance like a bear." Public attention is generally concentrated on standardized beauty such as the Grand Canyon, Yellowstone, and Yosemite. Lopez believes that a more dignified and enlightened approach is in order where a deeper understanding is generated for less spectacular regions. According to Lopez, "Unheralded landscapes are still part of the face of God."

As a boy growing up in southern California, Lopez was attracted to places like the Mojave Desert, which seemed on the surface to be simple. What he found was an important life lesson. That is, the person who looks plain, who at first glance is not so attractive, can be profound, deeply engaging, very complicated, and enthralling. The same holds true for landscapes. But even the most dazzling natural areas soon become ordinary without an excitement and longing to want more intimate contact with them.

It appears that the interest of most visitors to parklands is to act on the place. To Lopez this is a "narcissistic attitude" because the motivation is to perform in the landscape, not necessarily to appreciate the environment for more powerful, reflective reasons. Lopez admonished that a park is not a playground and that a resource does not have to be used to be valuable.

Coupled with the prevailing attitude that the worth of nature ultimately reduces to its entertainment value is the notion that interpreters should be entertaining. Under these circumstances it is difficult for interpreters to conduct their work, to maintain a sense of integrity. According to Lopez, the extensive use of videos and other media to satisfy the public's yearning for entertainment is a "morally bankrupt" approach to the interpretation of a place. Programs should not be designed to fill a void for visitors who come to a park expecting to be entertained. To become involved in a "circus performance" denigrates the interpreter's calling in life. Lopez acknowledges that the job of interpreters is enormously complex: "to undermine the complacency of how most people relate to the landscape." This can be accomplished only if interpreters work to their utmost potential.

Lopez believes that capturing the attention of the public is facilitated by the ability of interpreters to tell a story. A background in liberal arts "is essential because so much of the [interpreter's] work is dealing with metaphors." This grounding in the liberal arts allows interpreters to find appropriate metaphors that will engage the imagination of their audiences.

It is also desirable for interpreters to have a background in the natural sciences. However, this is less mandatory. It is noteworthy that Lopez had no university training in natural history. A strong, formal, liberal arts education (bachelors and masters degrees from the University of Notre Dame) gave him the skills to investigate natural history on his own, culminating in such works as Of Wolves and Men.

There is also a range of skills that interpreters could learn about and utilize from actors and writers in the realm of structuring, organizing, and presenting information. (The following essay will explore interpretive theater.)

Lopez also feels that there is much to be gained from reading extensively. He indicated that reading is valuable on three different levels. First, and most obvious, reading allows one to be exposed to factual and anecdotal information that may be used in interpretive programs. Second, reading allows the interpreter to observe how the written material is structured—what holds the material together. By paying attention to technical aspects of the written word, such as organizing principles or tone of voice, the interpreter can develop a more sophisticated style of delivery. Third, reading is what Lopez calls "part of the endless process of the discovery of the other." Because information can be construed in many different ways, extensive reading allows one to develop a broad picture from several different perspectives.

In addition to book knowledge, an interpreter's authority comes from personal experiences in a particular landscape. In Crossing Open Ground, Lopez suggests that close association with nature "speaks to a need many of us have but few can attend to—long-lived intimacy with a place, being able to speak of it knowledgeably to others." Lopez does not take this capacity for an intimate relationship with nature for granted. Our own quest to achieve a sense of place requires that we work diligently at it, daily. Lopez indicated that as a resident in a certain park you have to renew constantly your capacity for the complexity and wonder of the place. In practical terms what this means is that you "behave like a [native] hunter, always watching what is going on." Ultimately, a reciprocal relationship with the land is established in which you become aware that the landscape is aware of you. What can be achieved through this "erotic" bond is a spiritual dimension of the landscape which is subtle, complicated, and private.

Because interpreters generally know more about a particular landscape than the members of their audience, they are more familiar with the ways in which the landscape is imperiled. Interpreters should aspire toward "closing that gap between people and place." Freeman Tilden recommended, "exposing the soul of things—those truths that lie behind what you are showing your visitor." This may be partially accomplished through helping visitors create their own close relationship with the land. Lopez noted that in the Inuit dialect there is a word for "storyteller" that translates as "a person who creates the atmosphere in which wisdom reveals itself." This is the charge of the interpreter.

Lopez indicated that he strives to develop for listeners at his speaking engagements "a better sense of their own possibilities." Lopez suggested that interpreters should be concerned with this same sort of thing. The way to do this is to initiate direct contact with visitors, achieve a sense of intimacy with them, and serve as a role model.

Interpreters should demonstrate care, concern, and respect for visitors. They must have a "sense of compassion" for those people who are unfamiliar with natural environments. Although acknowledging some of the outrageous things that some visitors say or do, Lopez advised that telling "stupid visitor" stories, a form of catharsis, is counter-productive. Our challenge is to draw up in visitors those same qualities to which we aspire. Ultimately, park visitors should be made aware that they have the same potential to find worthy these natural landscapes, as we do.

Of course, this type of approach may not carry with some people; many cannot be reached. This faction, represented by a level of abuse and vandalism to the environment and disrespect for park employees, borders on, or evidences, mental illness. Still it is fruitful to encourage in visitors "a sense of self-love, self-respect, and self-worth" because it is out of these emotions that responsible behavior originates.

According to Lopez, the most effective message is that which is presented by example. People learn from representative aspects of the people they admire. In particular, as role models, interpreters present their quality of life as a result of staying close to the environment. This relationship, "marked by a depth of knowledge and a sense of wonder, serenity, and fulfillment" is something that visitors will notice. They may inquire, on a personal level, how the interpreter can achieve these qualities in life and they may, ultimately, try to emulate them.

To draw visitors into what you have to offer requires a humble approach. A self-effacing tone is more likely to engage an audience than a self-dramatizing or arrogant delivery. The interpreter should display a sense of respect for the landscape and a sense of respect for humanity. It is essential to introduce people to "something you love, not something you own."

Interpreters can convey this affinity for place by hinting that what they do isn't a job or occupation, but rather a way of life. The "calling is a high calling" that many in our society don't recognize.

There is a parallel, we think, between the work of a writer and that of an interpreter. On several occasions Lopez revealed that his life is devoted to language, ideas, and landscape. The life of the interpreter is similarly devoted, with perhaps less emphasis on language and ideas and more emphasis on landscape. But it is the degree of devotion that is telling. When Lopez says, "I'm a writer," he does so with a pride and conviction that reveals his full dedication to the craft. It is clearly apparent that he has deliberately chosen, and is committed to, his way of life. To be most effective, interpreters should feel this same passion for purpose. Lopez observes himself as a sensing element with a community obligation to share knowledge and experiences. To be involved in environmental interpretation carries a similar obligation.

Lopez believes that interpreters should ask themselves often, "What is the basis of my authority?" By assessing what makes it worth a visitor's time to listen to you, you discover the areas in which you need to work. Lopez suggested the importance of a mind that is always fresh enough to take in and be inspired by new knowledge and experiences.

On a different level, interpreters should be diligent in their preparations for interpretive events and in their clarity of presentation. Again there are parallels between writing about and interpreting landscapes. In an article that appeared in the Los Angeles Times Book Review, Lopez is quoted as saying that he makes "a bow of respect toward the reader." In paying respects to the reader, Lopez said, "I have assembled this material. I have tried to bring order to these disparate elements. I have tried to use the language elegantly. I have sought, everywhere I could, illumination, clarity. I have tried to organize things with a proper sense of the drama of human life; I have tried to think hard about all these things. I have tried to get rid of all that is unnecessary for you to understand the story." The interpreter owes this same degree of attention to the park visitor. Interpreters should strive for presentations that the audience will sense entailed a great deal of research, a great deal of thought, and a great deal of care. This type of approach to one's work requires substantial effort. But, it is only a concerted effort that has the potential to undermine the complacency of many park visitors.

Lopez summed up his respect toward the material in the following way: "Listen. Pay attention. Do your research. Try to learn. Don't presume. And always imagine that there's more there than you could possibly understand or sense." Interpreters owe this same level of deference to their interpretation of the cultural and natural history of their sites.

Lopez teaches, in part, through his own example. There is something admirable about how Lopez approaches his work. He indicated that he devotes so much of himself to his writing that he is in somewhat of an incoherent state after completing a manuscript. A lesser degree of intensity might be detected as a less engaging style of writing. Lopez mentioned on several occasions that he brings the integrity of his life to his work.

Of course, there is more to life than devotion to one's work, however noble. As a teenager, Lopez once listened to every New York Yankee game of the season on the radio. Although he is a devout sports fan he also exhibits a considerable knowledge about local, national, and international events. Lopez is anything but one-dimensional.

Beyond this, Lopez exhibits deep concern for others. He spoke frequently of his wife and friends. Basically, the message Lopez offers transcends the superficial. He said at one point that it is a "terrific struggle to be a decent human being." What he is getting at through his writing and through his actions is what it means to live well, with honesty and integrity. His deep concern for others was indicated in this recitation of a poem by a 12th-century Japanese monk at the close of his lecture to the university community.

On a mountain stream
A Mandarin Duck
Made single by the loss of its mate
Now floats quietly over riffles
A frame of mind I know.

Mandarin Ducks, Lopez explained, mate for life. So to see a single adult floating alone on a mountain stream is especially tragic. We can relate to the emotional hurt and emptiness felt when someone dear is lost. Lopez revealed, "It attracted me in some way I can't rightly say to this man who wandered as a monk. From these few words of translation I know [the poet] was a human being thinking about the same things we're thinking about. It also is worth remembering as a poem because in a simple way it closes this gaping wound between ourselves and the natural world."

Lee Stetson on Interpretation

Lee Stetson is a professional actor who has performed more than 50 major roles, from Shakespeare to Simon. He founded and managed the Hawaii Performing Arts Company and was the artistic manager of the Antique Theatre festival of Idaho. But he is best known in interpretive circles for his writing and performing of "Conversation with a Tramp: An Evening with John Muir" and his other Muir shows at Yosemite National Park. Stetson was interviewed for this essay, which focuses on the logistics of creating theatrical presentations and promoting environmental integrity through the arts. Stetson was asked many questions regarding the "ingredients" for an effective dramatic presentation. Perhaps this information may be used as a model for others who aspire to create similar interpretive productions.

Many years ago, Lee Stetson found himself in Los Angeles pounding the pavement and looking for work with 35,000 other actors. At the time he was exploring the southern Sierra and a friend sent him a biography of John Muir. Stetson relates, "I was immediately astonished by not only his incredible contribution to the environment, but also the poetry of his words." Stetson began exploring the possibilities of turning Muir's character into a theatrical production. He moved to Yosemite Valley and for seven months worked as a hotel desk clerk for the concessionaire while he completed his research. He walked in Muir's footsteps in Yosemite and steeped himself in Muir's letters, journals, and books. Then on April 21 (Muir's birthday) the first production opened at the visitor center in Yosemite National Park in 1983.

When asked about the writing phase of the Muir show, Stetson revealed that initially he wrote down all of the material that he felt was interesting, including phrases and whole stories. Then he put this together into subject matter categories and linked the bodies of material together and shaped them to come up with something that he thought was dramatic and interesting. He found that he had far too much material and eventually edited the show to be about one and a half hours in length.

An important aspect of the production was choosing the moment of time in which the action occurs. Stetson chose what he felt was the most dramatic context for the story, "when Muir was most down." The story takes place as Muir awaits President Woodrow Wilson's decision on the Raker Bill, which would authorize the construction of a dam in Yosemite National Park. This setting in time also provides for conflict or anticipation of some kind which motivates the audience to sit through the performance to find out the outcome.

Stetson believes that for the show to work it is important to get the most rounded character possible. In addition to reading all of Muir's works, Stetson also read every possible source of those who wrote about Muir to learn about his style of living. He notes the value of looking for aspects of the character's life that show the faults, foibles, and funny moments that all of us experience. Incorporating these aspects of the character helps to enrich the show enormously.

To provide an element of authenticity, Stetson also concerned himself with what a 75-year-old man is all about. Various artifacts (generally available in antique stores) can suggest the fullness of a person's life. Likewise, Stetson notes that attention to detail in developing costuming and props is essential. These accessories, according to Stetson, "often make a big difference and allow the character to shine."

Although Stetson seems adamant about portraying the integrity of a character ("the degree of sloppiness in this area is representative of that in other areas"), he believes that lighting and sound effects should be reduced as much as possible in park theater. In most parks, people are "trying to get away from the kaleidoscope of images that assail them in the city." Generally, Stetson is opposed to film, videos, and other audiovisual media in parks. He said, "I think there is a visceral connection between a live performer and the audience that is simply not available on the screen."

Stetson contends that it is not absolutely essential that interpreters have extensive dramatic training. He advises that the quality of acting is evidenced by the degree to which the character feels those things that are being portrayed. The preferred way to convey a message is for the character to show, rather than tell. There must be a commitment to delivering the joy, the anger, the overall passion of the character. Using the full gamut of emotions, from laughter to sorrow, is essential in eliciting a reaction from the audience. Stetson advises, "The character must be moved to expect the audience to be moved also." What is difficult, according to Stetson, is working on the acting techniques that allow one to become fully engaged in each and every moment. Furthermore, it is difficult for non-actors to sustain a show over a long period of time.

However, it is not necessary for interpreters to develop full-length productions from scratch. What is within the realm of most interpreters would be smaller projects that would not be as demanding in terms of research, script writing, dramatic skills, and time investment. This approach would allow interpreters to hone their skills over time and to continue adding short segments in the development of a larger production over, say, a couple years. Large park operations might also consider dramatic training for interpreters. Stetson believes that it is possible for interpreters to gain the expertise necessary for bringing theater into their parks.

The other possibility, of course, is to bring professional actors and actresses into the parks. Based upon his association with Yosemite, Stetson sees a logical future for arts in the parks—from theater to puppetry to storytelling to music. At Yosemite, the Muir shows are entirely self-supporting. In fact, beyond paying for Stetson's salary, a technician, promotion, and so on, the shows bring an infusion of surplus funds into the Yosemite Association to sustain other conservation efforts. The arrangement, then, has been tremendously successful at Yosemite. Stetson notes, "It seems to me very natural that we would want to put arts that are related to the environment in the parks, that there would be human-to-human contact, and that people will pay a minimal charge as long as they are assured a quality production."

The Muir shows have been so successful that Stetson was involved in developing a show about John Wesley Powell for Grand Canyon National Park. Although he doesn't perform the Powell character, he notes there are similarities between this show and the Muir productions. For example, both men confronted a growing America, both were involved in adventure and lived in the wilderness, both offered strong environmental messages, and both were basically ignored by the public during their time.

In addition to bringing theater into the parks, Stetson reflected on the connection between many art forms and protection of the environment:

> Not many of us, even those of us in the forefront of environmental battles, will tramp through the rainforest, or touch a whale, or listen to the wind play in the Arctic wilderness. But the images—the words, the sounds, the movements—of poets, painters, photographers, film makers, storytellers, puppeteers and musicians who are engaged in the battle for the unseen, the untouched, and the unheard can move us. This brings to many a temporary vitality, provides a sharing of one another's truth and especially reaffirms the possibility of creation. I am passionately convinced that art can serve to enhance our moral sensibilities and to promote in many a sense of environmental integrity. It used to be that our place on this planet was well claimed by the feelings of the people who lived here. Indigenous peoples, once naturally contained and nourished by the environment, integrated and celebrated that environment in their art, dance, music, and community rituals. Their daily art evoked their values, aspirations, understanding, and their thoughts. The things we still need to learn are very old things we once knew well.

Stetson acknowledges the power and transforming qualities of art to move people. The greatest insight he has gained from the study and character enactment of John Muir is the great hunger on the part of the public to hear a simple truth eloquently told. Ultimately Stetson emphasizes, "The arts are a medium for gentle awakening of the unconscious good people and we desperately need more unconscious good people becoming conscious."

3

Professionalism

Resolving the Interpreter's Identity Problem

As discussed in the foreword, the use of the term interpretation *for what we do and the term* interpreter *for those who do it has been controversial for decades. In this essay we offer straightforward suggestions for minimizing the confusion.*

There is often confusion among the public about what interpretation is or what interpreters do. This confusion has been a source of frustration for interpreters since the term gained wide-spread application to our profession in the late 1930s. For interpreters, the casual "What do you do for a living?" question defies a simple one-word answer like physician, attorney, teacher, engineer, or salesperson. Many interpreters have found that even their close friends, relatives, and immediate family members don't really understand the significance of the label that has been attached to our profession.

The public tends to perceive interpreters, mostly, as those who translate a foreign language. Of course, some park interpreters are fluent in other languages. And most major parks offer written and recorded interpretation in several languages! However, our primary duty is to interpret or translate a foreign environment—one that the visitor to the site is unfamiliar with. How can this distinction be conveyed to the visitors of our national heritage?

In the 1970s there was a movement within the profession proposing a slightly different spelling of the word interpreter designed to distinguish our field. Specifically, some proposed changing the normal spelling to "interpretor." A review of the early volumes of the Journal of Interpretation (late 1970s to the early 1980s) turns up several articles using this spelling. The spelling was even adopted by some natural resource agencies for their interpretive publications and internal communications. However, interest seemed to wane during the mid-to-late 1980s.

Then the issue of what to call ourselves, and how to spell it, was resurrected in the mid-1990s in a book on interpretive planning in which the term "interpretor" was used once again. The book includes a footnote that explains the purpose: "Throughout this text, the spelling interpretor is used to distinguish the profession from that of an interpreter (or translator) of foreign languages."

Although the altered spelling at first glance seems harmless enough, this is a complex issue that deserves considerable professional attention. We believe that the intent of all those using "interpretor" is admirable. That is, interpretation of cultural and natural resources is a noble profession that is distinct from foreign language interpretation and should be recognized as such. There are, however, several problems with the new spelling.

First, and most important, is that "interpretor" cannot be found in the dictionary. The word currently does not exist, at least in terms of its inclusion in any major reference work. So, only those who already know, somehow, that the new spelling refers to interpreters of cultural and natural history will understand the use. Everyone else will assume that the word is misspelled. And they still won't be able to make a distinction between what we do and what a foreign language interpreter does.

Second, interpreters are often accused of "preaching to the choir." To expand that analogy to this issue, in changing the spelling we are doing something even less worthwhile. We are preaching to other preachers! In other words you have to be one to "get it."

In essence, advocates of the new spelling are trying to force change upon the language. Interpreters are not the first or only group to attempt to change language in this way. William Zinsser, in On Writing Well, relates how certain feminist groups have been proposing use of unisex pronouns to encourage gender inclusive speech. These unisex pronouns are derived from Nordic or Anglo-Saxon roots. For example, one of the candidates for a new pronoun is "thon" a third-person pronoun that applies to either gender and is easily changed to other forms. However, as Zinsser points out, "I doubt that thon wants that word in thon's language or that thon would use it thonself." He adds, "That is not how language changes." Yet, some interpreters may be attempting similar linguistic gymnastics. Moreover, there is but a subtle difference in how the two spellings are (apparently) pronounced. That is, there is very little verbal distinction between interpreter and interpretor.

If changing the spelling isn't the answer, is it our professional destiny to have this identity crisis in perpetuity? We don't think so. As we now move well into the 21st century, several strategies if applied with a concerted effort over time could lead to a general adoption and understanding of the word, as we use it, by the public.

One useful practice would be to simply precede "interpreter" with the resource being interpreted (e.g., park interpreter, zoo interpreter, forest interpreter, etc.) This practice is common in sciences where the generic "biologist" is specified as a microbiologist, an evolutionary biologist, or a wildlife biologist.

Likewise, to enhance public understanding interpreters could, where the program is appropriate, discuss what we are called, what it is we do, why we do it, and the traditional confusion with our job title. This could well be educational and humorous depending on an interpreter's own personal experiences and approach to the topic.

Furthermore, signs at visitor centers, as well as other publicity, could specify what interpreters of our cultural and natural heritage do. This could be offered in conjunction with a concise interpretive mission statement for the site—widely available to the visiting public.

Of course, there is also the matter of various position titles within organizations. There are more than 30 different job titles for people who interpret, including rangers, guides, naturalists, and recreation planners, to name a few. Until we consistently call ourselves interpreters we can't expect the public to. Interpreters and professional organizations representing interpreters should encourage agencies to reassess these myriad titles and adopt a uniform title—interpreter—that reflects the unity of the profession.

Ultimately, our challenge is to interpret to the public what we do. In so doing we may foster support both for the intricacies of the profession and the settings where we provide interpretation. Given the nature of our work and our expertise as interpreters, we should be up to the task.

Becoming Better Interpreters

This essay, inspired by advice given by Barry Lopez, has been used by several states during their seasonal interpreter training sessions. It has served as the basis for a number of keynote addresses given at interpretation workshops.

In his book About This Life, Barry Lopez recounts a conversation with a passenger on an airplane. The passenger had discovered that Lopez was an accomplished author and sought advice for his 15-year old daughter who aspired to be a writer. Lopez offered the man three suggestions for his daughter. Specifically, Lopez said to encourage her to read, to travel, and to become someone. The advice given by Lopez is also applicable for interpreters seeking to reach their fullest potential.

Lopez's first suggestion was to tell the daughter to spend much time reading. Moreover, she should be encouraged to read whatever interests her, even if someone declares it to be trash. Lopez explained, "No one can fathom what happens between a human being and written language. She may be paying attention to things in the words beyond anyone else's comprehension, things that feed her curiosity, her singular heart and mind."

For many compelling reasons, interpreters too must read (as noted in a previous essay). Reading opens and expands the mind to new information, fresh ideas, and different perspectives. Reading inspires. The words of great writers stimulate readers to form their own new ideas. Reading causes interpreters to see things differently. For example, early-20th-century naturalist Mabel Osgood Wright referred to the American crow as "a feathered Uriah Heep." Anyone who has met Dickens' Uriah Heep in the pages of David Copperfield will smile knowingly at Wright's metaphor and may never interpret crows again in the same way. Reading such classics offers rich metaphors and examples that will illuminate interpretive themes and add meat to the thematic skeleton of any program or text.

Lopez instructed the father to encourage his daughter to seek out many different kinds of literary voices, speaking about universal themes like love, courage, sacrifice, commitment, and freedom. Such themes are the foundation of many interpretive programs. Listening to diverse voices and perspectives on these themes will improve the interpretation of them, even if the interpreter does not personally adopt these perspectives. Merely considering different perspectives will change interpreters and improve their interpretation.

In a most practical way, interpreters can learn from and emulate successful writers to expand their own vocabularies and writing skills. Good writers are good readers. Samuel Johnson reinforced this idea that reading improves writing when he criticized another author by saying; "He wrote more than he read." Interpreters must ask themselves if they have written (or spoken) more than they have read.

In addition to reading, Lopez told the father to encourage his daughter to travel. Although Lopez recommended travel, he was not just speaking of flying off to some exotic destination. Rather the advice was to "get away from the familiar." Lopez suggested "to learn another language, live with people other than her own, to separate herself from the familiar. Then when she returns, she will be better able to understand why she loves the familiar."

Travel changes people. Mark Twain astutely wrote, "Travel is fatal to prejudice, bigotry, and narrow-mindedness—all foes to real understanding." Travel not only promotes understanding, but it brings forth compassion. "Travel isn't just broadening, I've realized, but burdening too," wrote author Judith Stone, adding, "I carry these lives and places with me. But I'm grateful for the ballast; it's keeping me from tipping into total complacency." She notes that travel changes the way we shop, vote, donate, and, in short, live. It's human nature to care about places and people that we know. The more we travel, the more we care. The more we care, the better interpreters we will be.

Tennyson claimed, "I am part of all that I have met." If this is true for us, then to become the best possible interpreters, we must meet and become familiar with as many people and places as possible. We maximize these encounters through travels near or far.

The third piece of advice from Lopez was to become someone. Although mastering techniques for effective writing is important, Lopez said it is even more important to "find out what you truly believe."

Interpretation textbooks and workshops can teach interpreters much about communication techniques, but Lopez said to the father, "If she wishes to write well she will have to become someone. She will have to discover her beliefs, and then speak to us from within those beliefs. If her prose doesn't come out of her belief, whatever that proves to be, she will only be passing on information, of which we are in no great need."

When we become someone we develop our own unique style of writing and interpreting. William Zinsser observes that many people are impatient to find a style "as if style were something you could buy in a style store at the mall." He goes on to explain:

> There is no style store. Style is organic to the person doing the writing [or interpreting], as much as him as his hair, or, if he is bald, his lack of it. Trying to add style is like adding a toupee. At first glance the formerly bald man looks young and even handsome. But at second glance— and with a toupée there is always a second glance—he doesn't look quite right. The problem is not that he doesn't look well groomed; he does, and we can only admire the wigmaker's almost perfect skill. The point is he doesn't look like himself. This is the problem of the writer [or interpreter] who sets out to deliberately garnish his prose. You lose whatever it is that makes you unique.... Therefore the fundamental rule is: Be yourself.

Obviously agencies cannot have interpreters totally "being themselves" without coordination and oversight. But, within the broad goals of their interpretive plan, administrators would be wise to allow interpreters to communicate messages in their own way, consistent with their own beliefs and convictions. Interpreters "being themselves" will communicate more convincingly. Interpreters who know who they are and what they stand for will interpret with confidence and conviction. The sad alternative is to have talking heads reciting scripts of canned programs.

Interpreters interpret with the eyes of both the scientist and poet. The best interpreters introduce things they love to people they care about. Many writers, including Enos Mills and Freeman Tilden, point toward love and passion as essential ingredients in effective interpretation. Yet, love and passion are the most personal of all emotions. They can be exhibited only by individuals who are aware of who they are and confident in this identity.

Mahatma Ghandi said, "My life is my message." When we achieve consistency in the relationship between who we are as a person, our world view, and what we communicate to others through interpretation, it can lead to powerful and beautiful experiences for both the interpreter and the audience. Our lives can be our most effective interpretive message. Zinsser wrote, "Sell yourself, and your subject will exert its own appeal." To sell yourself, you must be yourself. You must be somebody.

As we reflect on Lopez's advice to read, to travel, and to be someone, we see that they are interrelated. Reading allows us to do armchair traveling into new worlds. Likewise, traveling exposes us to new writings, new voices. And, in turn, our reading and traveling allow us to encounter more people and places that define who we are as we become somebody.

Walt Whitman said the secret to making the best persons "is to grow in the open air, and to eat and sleep with the earth." No interpreter would argue about how nature nourishes us, but the secret of making the best persons (and the best interpreters) includes not only having fellowship with the earth, but with other humans as well. By reading about diverse human responses to our universe, by celebrating human creativity through the written word, by traveling into other landscapes physically or vicariously, by seizing new experiences and meeting new people, interpreters become inspired by the beauty of both nature and people. Interpreters then become somebody and use their own voices to inspire others. Reading, traveling, and becoming someone—not only do these things make us better interpreters, but better human beings.

4

Application

A Pocket Change History of the Lewis and Clark Expedition

This essay and the one that follows focus on using those things that surround us daily to better relate to our audiences and interpret our subject. These examples are intended to inspire other creative ideas for making emotional and intellectual connections between the interests of our audience members and the meanings inherent in the places we interpret.

The imagery that is placed on our currency—bills and coins—highlights those aspects of our cultural and natural heritage that our society identifies as being most important to us. Design changes to the 2004 and 2005 nickels reflect the value we place on the exploration of the United States at the time of Thomas Jefferson's presidency. The nickels can also be used as a brief lesson on the evolution of American attitudes toward the landscape, which will make up the latter part of this essay.

For 66 years, the design of the Jefferson nickel remained the same, front and back. In commemoration of the Louisiana Purchase and the Lewis and Clark expedition 200 years ago, a public law was enacted to modify the Jefferson nickel. For the year 2004, the front of the nickel remained the same, the profile of our third president that we are accustomed to seeing. The reverse of the nickel, which historically featured Monticello, would now have two new images related to westward expansion. Of course, since Jefferson was already on the nickel, this was the perfect coin on which to celebrate these events.

The first new nickel reverse shows a likeness of the "Peace Medal" commissioned for the Lewis and Clark expedition by Jefferson, featuring symbols of peace and friendship (a handshake below a crossed pipe and tomahawk). These medals were presented to Native American leaders as tokens of goodwill. Also, the words "Louisiana Purchase" are inscribed above the date of the purchase of that immense territory.

The second nickel reverse of 2004 shows a side view of the expedition's keelboat in full sail. The 55-foot keelboat, built to the specifications of Captain Lewis, could be sailed, rowed, poled like a raft, or towed from the riverbank. In the bow of the keelboat are Captains Lewis and Clark in full uniform.

The obverse (front side) of the 2005 nickels bears a new likeness of Thomas Jefferson, and the "Liberty" inscription is based on Jefferson's own handwriting. The first of the 2005 reverse sides features the American bison. Expedition journals described the bison that roamed the plains in huge numbers. The bison symbolizes the wildlife encountered and the wealth of scientific information gathered during the expedition, as well as a reminder of the significance of bison to Native Americans for food, clothing, and shelter.

The second reverse design shows a view of the Pacific Ocean, the goal of more than a year of hard travel. The scene surrounds an excited entry from the journal of Captain Clark on November 7, 1805, "Ocean in view! O! The joy!"

These four images on the reverse sides of the 2004 and 2005 Jefferson nickels commemorate the challenge, adventure, and wonderment of the Lewis and Clark expedition. The National Geographic IMAX feature of the "Great Journey West" notes that the expedition was the modern-day equivalent of taking explorers to the moon and back.

In addition to this summary of the journey of the Corps of Discovery, this nickel series can be used as a lesson on how Americans have shifted in how we think about and behave toward nature. Looking at the nickels in the order of their appearance provides a history of the conservation movement, although there is overlap among the various phases of our relationship with the landscape.

The first image represents expansion. The Louisiana Purchase in 1803 set the stage for the Lewis and Clark Expedition. The U.S. ambassador to France, Robert Livingston, and a special envoy, James Monroe, negotiated with Napoleon Bonaparte, whose treasury was depleted, and who needed funding for his military operations. They made the purchase from France, a territory extending from the Mississippi River to the Rocky Mountains, for $15 million. That amount of money, today, would buy a couple of nice homes near the coast in San Diego. At that time, the additional 820,000 square miles more than doubled the size of the United States.

The next image goes hand-in-hand with the first and represents exploration. The keelboat transported expedition members and their supplies through the rivers of the Louisiana Territory. Jefferson had long been interested in the West, including the geography, plants, animals, native peoples and their habits, and the potential for expanding the young republic. His vision is evident in his first inaugural address: "However our present interests may restrain us within our own limits, it is impossible not to look forward to distant times, when our rapid multiplication will expand itself beyond those limits and cover the whole … continent, with a people speaking the same language, governed in similar forms and by similar laws."

And so the republic was expanded and explored westward to the Pacific coast. What followed was a period of exploitation that is symbolized by the American bison. The historic numbers of bison were estimated to be in the range of 30–70 million. In less than a century (the 19th) the population had been reduced in numbers to less than a thousand and the bison was close to extinction. The carnage is but one example of exploitation as the country expanded. As one other illustration, close to 90 percent of the virgin forests in America had been cut by the end of the 1800s.

The last of the nickels, with a glorious view of the Pacific coastline, represents enjoyment, which is consistent with an evolving sense of appreciation for the landscape. This shift in attitudes toward our natural heritage is documented in many scholarly works such as Roderick Nash's classic, Wilderness and the American Mind. As Nash noted in the fourth edition of his book:

> After the psychologically important "ending" of the American frontier in 1890 … Americans were becoming civilized enough to appreciate wilderness. They could begin to understand it as an asset rather than as an adversary. Perhaps uncontrolled nature could be beautiful; maybe it was more appropriate for worship than churches; certainly it had a lot to do with American character and tradition, and, possibly, with mental health in an increasingly complex civilization.

Ideally, the 2004 and 2005 Jefferson nickels may inspire people to learn more about our westward expansion and the Lewis and Clark expedition as the bicentennial celebration of that great adventure passes. Furthermore, these nickels can be used to convey the changing American conception toward nature: from expansion to exploration to exploitation to enjoyment. Of course, enjoyment and appreciation of our cultural and natural heritage is relatively recent and still incomplete. The charge to us in the interpretive profession remains clear: to help guide people and provoke their interests—to forge emotional and intellectual connections—regarding the merits and joys of our heritage.

Interpreting Our States' Heritage

This essay won first place in the category of Outstanding Commentary from The Interpreter *magazine. It offers suggestions for application of the successful State Quarters Program in interpretation using the California quarter as a case study.*

A cardinal purpose of Interpretation, it seems to me, is to present a whole rather than a part, no matter how interesting the specific part may be.

—Freeman Tilden

This essay will address potential uses of the U.S. Mint's 50 State Quarters Program (1999–2008) in interpretive venues using the California quarter as an example. The Quarters Program added 50 new quarter reverses, five per year for a decade, based on the anniversary of each state's admission to the union and when it ratified the U.S. Constitution. Delaware was the first state to release its quarter and Hawaii the last. This was the first change in the quarter since the 1975–1976 bicentennial quarter.

In California, the competition for the design of the reverse of the quarter drew 8,000 entries. This was narrowed down, eventually, to five designs. The finalists all represented aspects of the cultural and natural history of the state as follows: a seascape with sun and waves, the Golden Gate Bridge, the giant sequoia, a miner panning for gold, and Yosemite Valley with John Muir.

The choice of each state's design goes to the governor, and Governor Arnold Schwarzenegger chose Yosemite Valley and John Muir. However, the governor was not completely satisfied with the image by Garrett Burke, who has worked for Warner Brothers, Disney, and Nickelodeon. Governor Schwarzenegger wanted to add the California condor and make the image of Muir larger, which comprises the final design. Governor Schwarzenegger said, "These three images will show California's wildlife, California's magnificent landscape, and our commitment to preserving the Golden State for generations." The date on the coin, 1850, is significant because California entered the United States on September 9, 1850, as the 31st state.

This design gives us much to celebrate and interpret concerning California's remarkable heritage. Obviously, there is much to say about the California condor, about the life of John Muir, and about the geology, botany, and zoology of Yosemite. These tangible aspects of California's heritage also open doors to explore deeper meanings such as hope, faith, and beauty.

The image of the condor, we believe, represents hope. The California condor once had a range that extended across much of North America, but by 1940 had been reduced to the coastal mountains of southern California. By the 1980s, the wild population consisted of fewer than 25 individuals due to loss of habitat and environmental hazards. The last condors were brought into conservation breeding programs at the San Diego Zoo's Wild Animal Park and the Los Angeles Zoo. The California condor population now numbers approximately 300 birds with about half successfully reintroduced into the wild. These magnificent birds have a wingspan of nine feet and may fly up to 150 miles a day in search of food. The condor image on the coin opens up opportunities to interpret the bird's feeding, breeding, roosting, and other behaviors, along with an incredible success story of saving a species from the brink of extinction.

The image of John Muir, we believe, represents faith. Muir exhibited a deep spirituality. He memorized much of the Bible. He immersed himself in the glory of God's creation and shared his experiences and observations with the world. Muir accomplished so much in his life one hardly knows where to begin. He was a naturalist, writer, speaker, scientist, activist, inventor, visionary, and leader. Volumes have been written about him. Perhaps most important, now, Muir offers for us a role model of commitment. We might all learn from his flair for adventure, his dedication to his cause, and his passion for the gift of life. He was a champion for those without a voice ("fellow mortals") and he expressed wonder for all things wild. As we study John Muir, we gain a sense that whatever the setbacks may be, good will triumph over evil.

The image of Half Dome in Yosemite Valley represents beauty. Consider the vast and remote High Sierra wilderness, the glacial valleys, the towering spires and domes, the spectacular waterfalls, the wildlife, the groves of giant sequoias, and the delicacy of the summer wildflowers. Muir wrote, "Everything is so inseparably united. As soon as one begins to describe a flower or a tree or a storm … up jumps the whole heavens and earth and God Himself in one inseparable glory!" Yosemite offers us a sense of peace and spiritual uplift that defies description. Yosemite is so beautiful it can make you cry.

This has been a brief exploration of the possibilities for using the California quarter in interpretation. Similarly, you can use your state quarter in setting the stage for the cultural or natural heritage that is celebrated in your state. (To see the designs of the quarters, and for more information about each state quarter, visit usmint.gov.)

Perhaps your state coin celebrates a person such as Helen Keller (Alabama) or Abraham Lincoln (Illinois), a place such as Crater Lake (Oregon) or Chimney Rock (Nebraska), an event such as the Corps of Discovery expedition (Missouri) or the first flight (North Carolina), or a species of wildlife such as the American bison (both Kansas and North Dakota). Can you use your state quarter as an overview of what is significant in your state and relate it to your own site?

Yet another possibility is to use the state quarters as part of an icebreaker at the beginning of a program. Do people know what is on the state quarter where your interpretive site is? What can you tell them about the meanings behind the design? How about people from out of state—can they identify what is on the back of their state quarter? (You may be surprised at how many can't!)

As we interpret what is celebrated on our state coins, we realize that each one is only a thread in the fabric that makes up the rich diversity of our national heritage, and this in turn is only a piece of a larger puzzle that makes up all the nations of the earth, and, then, that the earth is but a speck of dust in the universe.

Muir, whose passion for his beloved Yosemite was unparalleled, revealed an understanding of our place in the larger scheme when he claimed the following as his address: "John Muir, Earth-Planet, Universe." In the tradition of Muir, may we each focus on the special attributes of our own interpretive sites while recognizing the wonders of all that lies beyond.

5

Universal Concepts

What is the Essence of Our Professional Responsibility?

This essay was written to help interpreters better understand the basics of tangibles, intangibles, and universal concepts as used in designing meaningful interpretation. It is presented in the context of a National Association for Interpretation annual workshop and draws comparisons between our professional conferences and heritage interpretation.

I am wandering aimlessly in the desert—at the foot of red rock mountains, brilliant white clouds streaming through a muted blue sky—reflecting on the NAI National Workshop in Tucson, Arizona. I am having trouble leaving, so I have stopped my car by the roadside to bid farewell to the saguaro that so conspicuously define the landscape.

This has been a terrific conference for three reasons. First, the people; a conference is always an outstanding chance to meet new people and see old friends. Second, the place; it's always a pleasure to explore the local area, whether the conference is in Anchorage, Cleveland, or Washington, D.C. The Sonoran Desert surrounding Tucson is no exception. Third, the personal development; these conferences offer terrific opportunities to grow and to learn more about interpretation as a profession, how to better perform our work. In Tucson, I enjoyed the educational sessions and gathered many valuable resources at the exhibit hall. But there was one presentation in particular that inspired me and has me thinking right now.

The National Park Service Process of Interpretation breaks down a place into tangibles, intangibles, and related universal concepts. David Larsen, who led a session on this process, suggested we inventory these things at places we interpret. So I am doing that right now as I meander through desert bajadas—gently sloping outwash plains at the base of these colorful mountains.

Let's start with the tangibles. I am dwarfed by saguaro, huge anthropoid cactus stretching for the sky. I am also surrounded by creosote, cholla cactus, palo verde, mesquite, and ocotillo. The indigenous people of this region have for eons depended on these plants and the animal life they support. In this place is everything the traditional people need: grocery store, liquor store, hardware store, clothing store, sporting goods store, drug store, music store, and toy store. For example, native Tohono O'Odham Indians harvest the figlike fruits of saguaro. They eat them fresh and make jam, syrup, and, for their religious ceremonies, wine. Long, woody ribs support the enormous weight of the saguaro, like narrow staves of an elongated barrel. These have traditionally been used to build shelters and fences.

I notice deer tracks and scat as I continue my wandering. Other mammals that might be observed here include mountain lion, coyote, bobcat, javelina, and fox. All of these I saw at the Arizona-Sonora Desert Museum, a unique collection of animals that are showcased in this, their native habitat. I also hiked in nearby Saguaro National Park with colleagues Ted Cable and Mark Morgan, and saw some of the native bird life: cactus wren, Gila woodpecker, gilded flicker, American kestrel, and phainopepla. The phainopepla's name is derived from the Greek for "shining robe," in reference to the iridescent, blue-black plumage of the male. In warmer weather, I might see all sorts of fascinating reptiles: Gila monsters, western diamondback rattlesnakes, desert tortoises, and chuckwallas. The chuckwalla has an effective strategy to avoid predation. It wedges itself between rocks and then inflates its skin like a balloon, making itself almost impossible to capture. The native people have found these large lizards to be a delicacy. They outsmart the reptiles by poking them with a pointed stick until they pop. In sum, the tangibles include the plants, the animals, the rock formations—the ecosystem itself.

Next, I turn to categorizing the intangibles. The intangibles, in contrast to real objects, are abstractions but no less important than the tangibles. What intangible qualities does this place preserve? Here is a short list: nature, heritage, knowledge, values. The tangible aspects of the landscape—the cactus, the elf owl, the rain clouds—are links to broader meanings. The power of the resources we interpret comes from their capacity to reveal meanings, the intangible qualities of the place, those things that move our souls. The charge of the interpreter is to help make the connection between the tangible and intangible.

According to Larsen, "You can label a whole group of intangibles 'universal concepts' [because] they are relevant to almost everyone." The possibilities will be the same, by definition, at natural sites as well as cultural and historical sites. Examples of universal concepts include beauty, freedom, responsibility, and community. These are concepts that almost everyone can relate to, but not in the same way. To illustrate, everyone has his or her own individual concept of God. I suspect that many universal concepts also include their opposites: life/death, creation/destruction, health/disease, elation/despair, and good/evil.

To craft worthy interpretation, the interpreter should consider the tangibles at the interpretive site. Information about the tangibles lays the foundation for bringing in the intangibles, revealing the meanings of the site, and addressing one or more universal concepts. In sum, the interpreter creates separate lists of tangibles, intangibles, and universal concepts. The next step is to consider the audience at hand and weave a relevant interpretation of the place. Larsen suggests there should be a balance—too much focus on the tangibles could get boring, whereas too much emphasis on the intangibles could be perceived as patronizing or irrelevant.

Here: I am struck by the beauty and diversity of the place, in particular the saguaro. No two are alike. Each is unique as an individual, like you and me. I wind my way along the wash to the tallest saguaro in the neighborhood. I stand at the base, looking skyward up the trunk of a sentinel that stands as high as a four-story building and weighs upwards of eight tons. This strongman has two large upward-thrusting arms and three smaller appendages, the smallest the size of a cantaloupe. There are cavities high on the trunk excavated by gilded flickers and Gila woodpeckers that could serve as a home for many different species of birds. These cavities are used for both nesting and as a refuge from the heat of a summer's day or the cold of a winter's day. The holes can be up to 20 degrees cooler or warmer than outside. This giant cactus is like a narrow, upright apartment complex for birds. It provides a life-sustaining resource for other life forms within the natural community. Just as the saguaro represents a focal point for the Sonoran Desert ecosystem, interpreters serve as sentinels and as a vital resource for visitors who come seeking meanings at the places in which they work.

At eye level, I am looking at the mottled olive-green trunk. The spines (an inch long, stiff, and sharp) are arranged in tufts, like pin cushions, and ascend in vertical columns to the top. These spines discourage wildlife from seeking moisture from the cactus and may partially shade the plant and shield it from drying breezes.

The saguaro and other organisms found here are well adapted to drought and the extreme desert heat. Rain is sporadic, coming mostly in the summer and winter. When rain does come, the saguaro collects the water with a network of roots that sink only three feet into the earth yet extend laterally from the base of the monarch for up to 100 feet. After a single good rainfall, the roots may soak up some two hundred gallons of water, enough to last the saguaro for a year. During dry months, the diameter of the plant will shrink and collapse like an accordion.

The saguaro are well spaced as the result of competition for water, and as I look at them I consider the human needs of intimacy and distance, community and solitude—opposites that are necessary for our well-being.

I also reflect upon how the workshop I just departed will sustain me throughout the coming year. The workshop's opportunities for inspiration from professional fellowship, adventure of learning about and exploring a new place, and educational resources to follow up on, are to me like that one burst of rain to a saguaro.

Our workshops, it occurs to me, precisely mimic the interpretive experience. The opportunities we experience at our national workshop are the same opportunities available to those who visit our sites of natural and cultural heritage.

First, our interpretive sites offer opportunities for people to interact with the family and friends they came with or to meet new people. Next, there is the place. As interpreters, we play a part in this. We share our knowledge and love for the site where we work. We assist visitors in their inventory and understanding of the tangibles and then make links for them with intangibles and universal concepts. Finally, we send people off to make application of what they have experienced in their lives. And each of them will respond differently. Visitors are sovereign, meaning that they have authority in what they think and believe. Larsen indicated that effective interpretation is "successful in creating opportunities for the audience to form their own intellectual and emotional connections to the meanings and significance inherent in the resource." In that way, interpretation is profoundly personal; not everyone is inspired similarly.

So we engage each visitor's imagination, just as my own has been engaged, by a social experience, the beauty and dynamics of a place, and the intellectual and emotional component. If we are fully successful (and this depends as much on the visitor as it does on us), the visitor will conduct his or her own interpretation of the place. Such an episode will facilitate understanding of the site, yes, but will also provide greater clarity about personal values and one's obligation to the broader community.

I imagine everyone leaving this workshop that launches the 21st century inspired in different ways. I consider the impact of all of us going back and putting into practice new insights that have been inspired by our camaraderie, the stark beauty of the desert, and our intellectual and emotional responses to the gathering.

Now consider that impact multiplied as visitors to the places we interpret return to their day-to-day lives confident in positive social interaction, calmed by the natural beauty of a park or the lessons commemorated at a historic site, and inspired by their own intellectual and emotional conclusions. What universal concepts might be contemplated (freedom, beauty, love, liberty, justice), and what might the consequences of such contemplation entail? A more compassionate and joyous republic?

I am convinced even more than before that we can make a difference and we do make a difference at the deepest level of imagination and meaning. And here is something reassuring. We don't do it alone. There are so many others who are involved with similar messages of inspiration and hope, both for humans and the broader natural community.

At a time when it is absolutely necessary, we are making a difference in the world. Bill McKibben, on the frontispiece of Environmental Careers in the 21st Century, wrote:

> Between now and 2050 we'll see the zenith, or very nearly, of human population. With luck we'll never see any greater production of carbon dioxide or toxic chemicals. We'll never see greater species extinction or soil erosion. So it's the task of those of us alive right now to deal with this special phase, to squeeze us through these next fifty years.

Those of us in the interpretive profession are on the front lines. It's not luck that will drive our success but, rather, hard work fueled by a sense of privilege for what we do. We help people better understand the tangible qualities of our cultural and natural heritage while pointing them toward the intangible values and universal concepts of the human heart and spirit.

Wicked Interpretation: Lessons from Broadway

This essay was written to help interpreters better understand universal concepts as used in designing meaningful interpretation. It offers insight about the power of musical theater and interpretation, both of which employ tools of voice, movement, music, props, and storytelling to reveal deep meanings that touch our hearts. This essay has been used by national consultant Stephanie Weaver in her "Creating Great Visitor Experiences" workshops.

wick-ed adj. Slang. Strikingly good, effective or skillful.
(The American Heritage Dictionary of the English Language)

Musical theater is in the arena of those things in life that are so influential they may transform us. These profound experiences may shift one's world view, one's sense of self, one's career or life trajectory. To paraphrase the NAI definition of interpretation, musical theater offers an experience that forges emotional and intellectual connections between the interests of the audience and the meanings inherent in the drama.

At the root of theater—and heritage interpretation—we may find underlying universal concepts that are relevant to almost everyone. These universalities include beauty, morality, freedom, gratitude, and love.

The application of universal concepts in interpretation has been gaining favor. Our interpretive sites give people access to universal meanings. The role of the interpreter is to make a link between the tangible resource and universal concepts; those meanings we can all relate to, those meanings that permeate and define human experience. People long to connect with the natural world and relate to our past in deep and powerful ways.

Interpretation of our natural heritage may focus on universal concepts such as change, survival, or diversity. Giant sequoias, for example, are symbols of stability, grandeur, complex interrelationships within community, and the silver lining of adversity. In the midst of a grove of giant sequoias we are humbled and exalted at the same time. We learn about our incomparable natural landscape and we learn about ourselves.

At historic sites the emphasis may be on meanings such as integrity or courage. These places celebrate the drama of human conduct. An awareness of our past gives us a fuller understanding of who we can be as individuals and as a community. For example, the life of John Adams, our second president, speaks to us of ambition, knowledge, civic responsibility, and faith.

A full spectrum of universal concepts can be found in theater such as: morality ("Wicked"), independence ("Mamma Mia"), tolerance ("Rent"), power ("The Lion King"), transformation ("Beauty and the Beast"), prejudice ("Hairspray"), war ("Little Women"), fear ("Phantom of the Opera"), dedication ("Jersey Boys"), and deception ("Dirty Rotten Scoundrels"). Note that there are generally three or more universal concepts in each production. Also note that "love" is a commonality that extends across almost all musicals. These and other universal concepts may be applied in heritage interpretation.

One of the hottest shows on Broadway and now also traveling the country is "Wicked: The Musical." It is the heretofore "untold" story of the witches of Oz. The original star of the show, Idina Menzel, won the Tony award for her portrayal of Elphaba, the Wicked Witch of the West. The show is a prequel to the Wizard of Oz series by L. Frank Baum (note el-pha-ba).

"Wicked" is playing at the Gershwin Theatre. I took my 14-year-old son, Spencer, to see Ms. Menzel during her last week of performance there. His passion is theater and his favorite actor is Ms. Menzel. We took a flight from San Diego for a five-day trip to New York City. Due to the extreme demand to see "Wicked," I secured tickets months in advance.

The Gershwin Theatre is magnificent in its size and clean lines. As you walk in the doors you are immersed in the fantasy to come. In the lobby there is an enormous map of Oz on the wall, as well as exhibits from the sets. The theater itself establishes a sense of place associated with the stage drama. As you leave the theater there are thematic messages above the exits.

The musical was everything my son dreamed of and more. The entire cast is superb, the sets are imaginative, the costumes are ostentatious, the music is inspiring, and the special effects are hypnotizing.

The meanings inherent in the drama are complex and touch on altruism, betrayal, vengeance, justice, and evil. A powerful thread woven throughout the production is the paradox of intimate friendship; how we are bound to hurt each other in ways that break the bond—or bring us closer together.

Usually there is a delay before a standing ovation, but in this case the audience was up and clapping before the curtain call could even begin. Next, Spencer wanted autographs. We asked where we could find the stage door and were told to look for the crowd gathered behind the police barricades. (I don't like crowds. I don't like waiting in line. I don't like standing in the cold rain late at night. But this was crucial for my son.)

Spencer was about three-deep in the mob as I wandered the perimeter of several hundred people. As the actors came out and signed programs, before climbing into limousines and being whisked into the night, I noticed that the fans who boldly held out their programs got them signed. I worked my way close to Spencer to offer some strategy. He is a tall kid and therefore was able to reach forward to get his program signed by most of his favorite cast members. The last actor to emerge was Ms. Menzel and Spencer was among the few to get an autograph to his sheer delight.

Over the course of our trip we explored Times Square, walked in Central Park, and saw several other musicals. At the airport, as we were waiting to go home, Spencer told me, "Dad, those were the best five days of my life."

In the profession of interpretation we explain something that we know about and have come to love to those who have less knowledge of, and affinity for, the subject. Ideally, we offer a story that people may relate to. My intent has been to guide you into a world you may be unfamiliar with and to offer associations with the broad mandate of interpretation.

Those of us in the profession of heritage interpretation are in a similar business as those who perform on Broadway. Our mission is to convey deep meanings that members of the audience may connect with. We use tools of voice, movement, music, props, and storytelling to reveal universal concepts.

Just as Broadway musicals may be awe-inspiring and transformational so are the places we work. As with the theater I described, we can create within our interpretive centers a sense of welcome and wonder. We can project a sense of place, of being somewhere special. Interpretive center design and the exhibits therein are instrumental in connecting people with the sacred places that make up our cultural and natural heritage.

Furthermore, we can make ourselves available to people. There is no telling how much this may influence a person's experience. An entire line of research has been initiated in hospitality and tourism management that deals with "supplementary service." How we treat our visitors does make a difference. We can also seek ways for visitors to take with them a memento of the visit that extends the meaning of the experience. The theater program ("playbill") and signatures that Spencer collected will afford precious memories for years to come and a reconnection with the meanings he absorbed.

Most important will be making application of universal concepts in such a way that audiences will connect to the meanings inherent in the resource. We can help guide people to make associations between the tangible resources and the meanings they represent.

One's response to theater, or good interpretation, may elicit deep emotions, generate a sense of truth, foster consideration of new priorities, assist in confronting adversity, initiate a generous response, inspire a courageous course of action, or encourage a less complex, less stressful, less consumptive way of life. The reaction to theater or interpretation may also brighten one's outlook, provide a sense of hope, or momentarily overwhelm the senses. Rick Elice, the co-author of Jersey Boys, said, "A good musical can make you thank God for the day you were born."

What did I gain, what meanings struck a resonant chord, from this trip to New York City with my son? Far more than can be conveyed in this short essay. But, overall, whatever the cost may have been it was worth it for those words I heard from Spencer at the airport. We only have one shot on this planet. We can help make the dreams of others come true (as actors, as interpreters, as parents) and in so doing we see our own dreams come true.

> Dancing through life, down at the Ozdust / if only because dust is what we come to.
> And the strange thing, your life would end up changing / while you're dancing…through.
>
> —"Dancing Through Life," Wicked: The Musical

Global Interpretation

6

The Role of Interpretation in International Tourism

Interpretation is a noble profession that has global impacts in promoting conservation and peace. This essay has served as the basis for keynote addresses given at interpretation workshops.

In Nature's ennobling and boundless scenes the hateful boundary lines and the forts and flags and prejudices of nations are forgotten. Nature is universal. She hoists no flag of hatred. . . . He who feels the spell of the wild, the rhythmic melody of falling water, the echoes among the crags, the bird songs, the winds in the pines, and the endless beat of the waves upon the shore, is in tune with the universe. And he will know what human brotherhood means.

—Enos Mills

Tourism is the largest and the fastest-growing industry in the world. Virtually every country in the world and every state and province in North America is making a strategic effort to attract tourists. Their motives are mostly economic because tourism has the potential to generate new revenue and jobs. Futurist John Naisbitt predicted that "the 21st century economy will be driven by three super service sectors: telecommunications, information technology, and travel and tourism."

As tourism flourishes, opportunities for interpretation abound. Interpretation programs, products, and services now exist in most tourism destinations. Interpretation in the international tourism sector traditionally has been associated with destinations such as national parks, large museums, historic villages, and battlefields. Now many tourism destinations, including beachfront hotels, cruise ships, theme parks, and ski resorts offer interpretive services. Tourists in every major city in the world can find multilingual interpretive bus tours operated by private sector firms with guides trained to communicate their knowledge of the place. In some cities, such as London, city tour guides must be certified to ensure that their knowledge of the history, architecture, and local culture is adequate and that they have the skills to communicate this information in an entertaining manner.

The fundamental principles of interpretation apply regardless of whether the interpreter is working with tourists or residents in Timbuktu or Topeka. On the international scene, a heritage interpreter often needs also to be a foreign language interpreter. But, whether locally or internationally, interpreters always are interpreting meanings in things that are foreign—whether the language of the French or the language of the forest. Likewise, the benefits that individuals receive from interpretation are similar regardless of the location. Interpreters meet the personal needs of people in countless ways while touching their emotions and intellect. Interpreters give the gifts of joy, knowledge, beauty, and inspiration to all audiences, whether tourists or local guests. In the tourism sector, interpretation functions in a particularly wonderful way to enhance what might be a once-in-a-lifetime experience.

Beyond the direct benefits to individuals in interpretive audiences, the role that interpretation plays in manufacturing high-quality tourism experiences is profoundly important on a global scale. This essay describes the significance of interpretation as it promotes biological conservation and world peace in the context of international tourism.

Promoting Conservation

Conservationists and policymakers in many countries are attempting to attract tourism and use it as a tool to save natural areas. This approach is not new. Tourism played an important role in the justification and establishment of the early U.S. national parks and it is still being used as a conservation tool today. This natural resource-based tourism is often referred to as ecotourism. The International Ecotourism Society succinctly defines ecotourism as "responsible travel to natural areas that conserves the environment and improves the well-being of local people." Ecotourism is one of the fastest-growing sectors within the tourism industry. In recent decades, the growth rate of tourism has been greater in developing countries. Richly diverse, but highly threatened biological resources often characterize these countries. Conservation faces many complex economic and political challenges in developing countries. Ecotourism is seen as one approach to saving these resources while contributing to the welfare of the local people.

The fundamental basis for ecotourism as a conservation tool is to provide an economic incentive for people to protect their natural resources. Harvested resources—whether timber, grass, monkeys, or elephants—all have important values to local people, many of whom may be subsisting directly on the harvest of these resources. People cannot be expected to forego this harvest without alternative resources or income being provided for them. The task is to make the elephant worth more alive than dead, and the living forest worth more than the logs it contains. Then alternative sources of food or income must be provided to the people.

Ecotourism can save resources and bring prosperity to people. When it works well, ecotourism can benefit the local people and the host nation by bringing in foreign revenue through the payment of fees and the purchase of local goods and services (e.g., permits, fuel, food, guide services, lodging). Tourism is a labor-intensive industry and the provision of the goods and services results in the creation of jobs. Besides generation of jobs and revenue from expenditures, ecotourism can result in significant donations from altruistic tourists who are exposed to the conservation needs in areas they visit. Firms that profit from helping people experience these natural resources also contribute to the cause of conservation.

An example of excellence in this regard is the Galapagos Conservation Fund (GCF) established by Lindblad Expeditions, a travel company based in New York City. According to Dr. Sam Ham, communications campaign designer and trainer for the GCF project, $3.6 million has been raised to support conservation on the Galapagos Islands. Lindblad also works closely with and makes contributions to such groups as World Wildlife Fund and RARE Center for Tropical Conservation, an organization involved with developing ecotourism opportunities around protected areas in Latin America.

Some "green" travel businesses build contributions directly into the cost of their excursions. Other firms solicit additional financial or in-kind donations from their clients for nature conservation. For example, Wilderness Birding Adventures encourages clients participating on bird watching trips in Alaska to make a $1 per day contribution to the Alaska Bird Observatory, the Northern Alaska Environmental Center, or the Alaska Conservation Foundation. This donation is conveniently figured into the client's bill. This firm also makes a 10 percent donation to the American Birding Association on selected bird-watching tours.

Besides direct financial contributions, ecotourism sometimes benefits local people by contributing to the development of community infrastructures. Ecotourism organizations provide new bridges, clinics, water wells, electricity, schools, and other assets to help local communities, particularly as they prepared for an influx of travelers for the first time.

How can interpretation enhance the conservation benefits of ecotourism? Interpretation as part of ecotourism experiences contributes to conservation on several levels. By making the tourism experience more enjoyable, educational, and enriching, interpreters increase the value of the experience. Just as with other market commodities people may be willing to pay more or consume more when the product is perceived to be of high value. In this way, interpretation can encourage demand and keep the resultant revenue flowing into the host country and local communities. Moreover, a fundamental principle of interpretation is that it should provoke thought or action. Inspiring and convincing interpretation can provoke political support and donations of time and money for the cause of conservation in these locations. Once-in-a-lifetime, possibly life-changing world-class experiences turn the heart of the tourist toward helping.

An interpreter who assigns meaning and significance to the natural resource may prompt gifts of appreciation for preservation. Also, as local guides and interpreters are hired, interpretation creates jobs and income for local families. These jobs, along with the modeling of environmentally responsible behavior and the interpretive messages being communicated, can build support for conservation among local people. When people understand that they have something unique and valuable to offer the rest of the world, they often take pride in their natural and cultural heritage and want to protect those resources for future generations.

If people in modern industrial countries want to preserve nature in poor developing countries, they are going to have to pay for it themselves. Ecotourism provides a revenue-producing product and one framework for delivering payments to fund conservation efforts. Interpretation can enhance the tourism product, promote stewardship among local people and tourists, increase understanding and concern about conservation needs, and provoke expenditures and philanthropy.

Like any powerful tool, ecotourism only works in certain situations. It is not always the appropriate conservation approach. Ecotourism can damage natural resources and local communities if it is used unwisely. Infrastructure developments and the increase in people can pollute or totally eliminate the very ecosystems tourism was meant to save. Crime, disease, loss of traditional family roles and values, and other social problems result from misguided ecotourism efforts. Leakage of the economic benefits out of the host community by not purchasing local supplies and services, or not hiring local guides and other labor, drains away the promised financial benefits.

To address these issues, travel industry associations, nature conservation groups, and international organizations such as the United Nations have established codes of ethical standards and codes of professional conduct to guide ecotourism providers and tourists. Countries such as Costa Rica, Kenya, and Australia have developed their own standards to reduce the negative impacts and maximize the benefits of ecotourism. For example, general standards from The International Ecotourism Society state that ecotourism should:

- Minimize impact
- Build environmental and cultural awareness and respect
- Provide positive experiences for both visitors and hosts
- Provide direct financial benefits for conservation
- Provide financial benefits and empowerment for local people
- Raise sensitivity to host countries' political, environmental, and social climate

Interpreters are distinctly positioned to achieve those aspirations and purposes. Interpreters teach people to travel softly with fewer negative impacts on the resource. They create positive experiences and their messages can raise awareness, respect, and sensitivity for cultures and their environments. As previously mentioned, interpreters can generate cash flow from expenditures, wages, and philanthropy for the benefit of local people and conservation.

Jacques Cousteau said, "People will only protect what they love." Interpreters help tourists see the beauty and value in landscapes, organisms, artifacts, and history. Like romantic matchmakers, interpreters bring together resources and tourists, create the appropriate mood, and raise levels of understanding and sensitivity to draw people closer to the resources and ultimately to learn to love them. If tourists care about the natural and cultural resources in places they visit, they will care for them. In this way, interpreters help maximize the conservation benefits and minimize the negative impacts of this growing industry.

Promoting Peace

The world is becoming a global village in which people from different continents are made to feel like next-door neighbors. In facilitating more authentic social relationships between individuals, tourism can help overcome many real prejudices, and foster new bonds of fraternity. In this sense tourism has become a real force for world peace.

—Pope John Paul II

Tourism has been called "The World's Peace Industry." In 1988, The First Global Conference: Tourism—A Vital Force for Peace was held in Vancouver, Canada, to explore "new initiatives to further the goal of global peace through tourism." The premise of the conference was that "tourism transcends governmental boundaries by bringing peoples of the world closer together through understanding of different cultures, environments and heritage."

As the Cold War of the late 20th century was nearing an end, President Reagan gave a speech in which he said of the United States and Soviet Union, "Imagine how much good we could accomplish, how the cause of peace would be served, if more individuals and families from our respective countries could come to know each other in a personal way…." A few days later Secretary Gorbachev and President Reagan issued a joint statement saying, "There should be greater understanding among our peoples and to this end we will encourage greater travel." Since the mid-1980s "peace through tourism" initiatives have expanded across the world, including many regional and global conferences. The Society of American Travel Writers (satw.org) Peace Through Tourism Committee and organizations such as the International Institute for Peace Through Tourism (iipt.org) foster tourism to bring about a peaceful and sustainable world. Indeed, many such efforts are underway to make tourism the world's first and foremost peace industry.

The value of travel in bringing people together has been recognized for many years. Travel reshapes the mind of the traveler. As author Judith Stone wrote (quoted in an earlier essay), travel can also be burdening as we develop a personal attachment to a place. It is not merely the physical movement of travel that brings forth the broadening and burdening. Rather, it is the illumination of the meanings and beauty of places and peoples that eliminates prejudice, bigotry, and complacency. This illumination is the goal and responsibility of interpreters in the tourism sector.

We care more about places and people we know. We skim over and barely notice news of an earthquake, tsunami, flood, or train wreck in a far-off land unless we have a personal attachment to that place and those people. Interpreters introduce tourists to new cultures and help them know the people. Interpreters touching emotional chords in the hearts of tourists evoke empathy for the local people and appreciation of their culture.

Of course, tourism is not always a unifying and enriching experience for the local hosts. Some communities and cultures do not welcome tourists. Some resent "rich tourists" walking through their villages spreading diseases and disrupting traditional village life. Tourism operators must be sensitive to the needs and desires of the host community. In this regard, The World Tourism Organization's "Code of Ethics" includes the following:

- The understanding and promotion of the ethical values common to humanity, with an attitude of tolerance and respect for the diversity of religious, philosophical, and moral beliefs, are both the foundation and the consequence of responsible tourism; stakeholders in tourism development and tourists themselves should observe the social and cultural traditions and practices of all peoples, including those of minorities and indigenous peoples, and recognize their worth.

- Tourism activities should be conducted in harmony with the attributes and traditions of the host countries and in respect for their laws, practices, and customs.

- Tourism activity should be planned in such a way as to allow traditional cultural products, crafts, and folklore to survive and flourish, rather than causing them to degenerate and become standardized. Local populations should be associated with tourism activities and share equitably in the economic, social, and cultural benefits they generate, and particularly in the creation of direct and indirect jobs resulting from them.

Interpreters contribute to each of these ethical standards by promoting understanding and appreciation of the beauty and value of diverse cultures. Interpreters help tourists to care about the welfare of the individuals, communities, and cultures they encounter in their journeys. As with natural resources, if tourists care about the people and cultures, they will care for them. In this way interpreters maximize tourism's potential for peace.

In sum, interpreters give gifts of understanding and beauty to travelers around the globe. These gifts have profound effects on the lives of tourists, as well as on the communities and countries hosting the travelers. These interpretation-driven changes in people foster the spread of stewardship and fellowship. Because of its ability to change human attitudes and behavior, tourism has been touted as a conservation tool to save nature, and has been called the ultimate peace industry. By communicating the values of natural and cultural heritage, interpreters enhance the benefits of international tourism. Interpreters, while enriching lives of travelers, assist them to be compassionate—assist them to care. Caring travelers contribute to conservation and peace. It is the privilege and the responsibility of interpreters to be conservation-makers and peacemakers throughout the world.

Blessed are the peacemakers. —Matthew 5:9

VolunTourism: Seeing the World and Saving the World

The realm of volunteer travel offers unique opportunities for travelers to gain deeper experiences while making the world a better place, with implications for interpreters and the field of interpretation.

One of the most exciting trends in world travel is the interest of tourists in enjoying the novelty of a different culture and land, while at the same time providing help to local communities. Many travel groups (such as Globe Aware) provide opportunities to combine travel and volunteerism. Volunteer excursions typically last anywhere from several days to several weeks—and you do have to pay for such experiences. However, trip expenses are tax deductible.

Such trips may attract individuals, couples, friends, and entire families who wish to spend their vacation time helping others in the United States and around the world. Volunteer work that is performed may include building homes, assisting medical centers, providing care at orphanages, or teaching English.

This approach to travel provides firsthand experience and could be an ideal way for interpreters to learn more about the cultures and landscapes of the world (as advocated in an earlier essay titled "Becoming Better Interpreters") while giving back to communities in need. Furthermore, interpretation can play a major role in VolunTourism by integrating opportunities for travelers to learn more about new cultures and landscapes through application of interpretive principles.

The term voluntourism (with a small "t") was first used by the Nevada Board of Tourism in 1998 to recognize volunteers who promoted the state of Nevada as a tourist destination. In 2000 there was a different movement that sought to combine the nonprofit sector and the tourism sector, with the name of VolunTourism.

David Clemmons is the founder of this concept and voluntourism.org and he is at the forefront of promoting voluntary service through tourism. VolunTourism is defined as a seamlessly integrated combination of voluntary service to a destination and the best traditional elements of travel—arts, culture, geography, and history—in that destination.

A powerful aspect of VolunTourism is that people are able to really connect with those of the host culture whom they are serving. This approach is unlike traditional tourism, where contact with the host culture is often limited to monetary exchanges for goods or services. With VolunTourism the host culture recognizes that people had reasons to visit in order to help. Furthermore, the host people and their children are exposed to other cultures, as well, and this is very meaningful to them.

Research has indicated that host cultures want to be involved with the assistance they receive. So, rather than having random levels of assistance (however well-intentioned) imposed on the culture, the local residents become players in the decision-making process. In other words, the local community determines the projects that are designed to help them.

The fact that people are coming to serve (in ways the host culture has determined will help them) creates considerable gratitude and trust in those being helped. And this level of trust means they will "open up" to those who have come to help them. When tourists are trusted at such a high level, the host culture will readily expose them to the more "sacred" elements of their culture.

The benefits of this approach to tourism are remarkable. The host culture is assisted in meaningful ways, and that culture is exposed to people coming from "worlds away" to assist them. The tourists involved help make the world a better place, while at the same time having unique and extraordinary experiences in places they have never been. Unlike mass tourism, VolunTourism allows intimate contacts with the hosts to occur. VolunTourism truly benefits everyone involved.

For prospective VolunTourists, Clemmons recommends a step-by-step process. First, you should identify the purpose of your VolunTourism experience. Why, exactly, would you be interested in this type of travel alternative? Second, you should assess your capabilities to determine the type of service you might best provide. What are your strengths and interests that might fit with a certain destination? Third, you should consider some tough questions. What are your minimum requirements for accommodations? What percentage of your overall time do you want to devote to voluntary service and to traditional sightseeing? How sensitive are you to poverty and starvation? How great is your tolerance for extremes in climate? What food preferences and aversions do you have? This type of assessment is very important in determining location and type of service.

With careful preparation and planning you can assure yourself of having the best experience possible. Clemmons suggests learning as much as you can about the culture you will be assisting. Many books and data-bases reveal cultural "dos" and "don'ts" for visiting a new place.

The following illustrations offer a small sampling of possibilities from around the world. In the town of Brasov, Romania, volunteers help ethnic minorities learn English, math, basic hygiene, and other life skills, as well as make infrastructure improvements in homes in the community. In Jamaica, volunteers work with a local nonprofit to promote ecotourism. Projects may include cleaning up local rivers and caves, marking trails, and controlling erosion on hillsides. In villages in Ghana, volunteers help by building schools, libraries, and Internet training centers, as well as constructing water systems that may save lives during droughts. In Cuzco, Peru, volunteers help educate children who come from families in the rural mountains who are too poor to care for them. In all cases, volunteers also have ample opportunities to see the local sights—like Machu Picchu in Peru, one of the wonders of the world.

VolunTourism offers deep and powerful opportunities to connect with host cultures and to help them, while simultaneously seeing the sights of new and exotic places. This approach to tourism, in which we transform ourselves through helping others, could truly change the world.

7

Inspiration

Interpretive Lighthouses

This short essay won an award from NAI Region 6 for Best Newsletter Article. Subsequently it was reprinted in other NAI newsletters and state interpretation publications.

Lighthouse.n.:atowerorotherstructurelocatedatsomeplacedangerousorimportantwithapowerful light that gives a signal for guiding travelers.

Explorers and settlers referred to the Great Plains as an ocean—a sea of grass. The wide horizons and treeless expanses were as daunting to these travelers as the Atlantic Ocean was to those who had crossed it in earlier journeys. Settlers hesitated at the shores of these regions before mustering the courage to set off across this ocean in their oxen driven vessels. Some attached sails to their wagons and tried to sail across these arid seas.

Millions of travelers still sail among this region's wind-swept waves of grass and grain. Sailors in air-conditioned cars speed through unfamiliar spaces. Some travel aimlessly, oblivious to the environment around them. Some sail through the seas on maiden voyages, others have sailed these seas for years. Many visitors wash up on our shores by accident. Others, keen explorers longing to see new places, arrive purposefully.

To sailors everywhere, especially those in sailing strange seas, lighthouses are beacons of comfort and security, guidance and hope. Everyday people "wash up on your shores" regardless of where you interpret. That is why it is so wonderful that "lighthouses" exist. Lighthouses, such as nature centers, zoos, museums, and historic sites that guide people through sandy pine forests, limestone glades, estuaries, reservoirs, cypress swamps, dry rocky steppe, and those oceans of grass called prairies.

Interpreters care for places that provide a sense of place and a sense of security. Interpreters see to it that their lighthouses effectively illuminate the surroundings. Interpretive sites also warn of dangers, and for confused or discouraged travelers they mark the route to safe harbors.

Since the 19th century, lighthouses have had what are known as Fresnel lenses. These lenses increase the power of the light and focus it in one direction. According to a PBS documentary on the subject, a Fresnel lens is "an elaborate orchestration of an array of lenses and dozens of prisms. Each piece is molded, polished, and set precisely to redirect diffuse lamp light into a unified far-reaching beam." Is that not what nature centers and other interpretive facilities seek to accomplish? Are not the best interpretive sites an elaborate orchestration of media and individuals molded, polished, and set precisely to direct unified far-reaching beacons of information and inspiration? Individually each interpreter at an interpretive site is a single lens contributing to a beam of light that is far-reaching and focused. Each interpreter works with other "lenses" to project unified interpretive themes deep into the hearts and minds of people passing by.

Lighthouses and interpreters are wonderful sources of encouragement to misguided, untrained, confused, oblivious, or fearful people. They are most needed in dark stormy times to guide people away from danger and keep them sailing safely and joyfully. Each day it is our responsibility, privilege, and pleasure to light our world.

The Need for Interpretation: Now More Than Ever

This essay was written immediately after the September 11, 2001 terrorism attacks.

In light of recent events, some of our students and colleagues have wondered about the appropriateness and relevance of interpretation in the face of overwhelming tragedy. An interpretive talk, historic site tour, or nature walk may appear trivial or mundane in the bigger picture of life and death. Many Americans are struggling with feelings of anxiety, fear, anger, and confusion. Where does interpretation fit in? What do the events of September 11, 2001, mean to the American people, and the people of the world? What are the implications in the short-term and what about the distant future? We believe the current circumstances make interpretation not less important, but more important than ever before.

Interpreters are stewards of the very places that make America special. Collectively, we tell the story of America. It is our work to interpret the cultural and natural treasures that define our nation. The places where we interpret are symbols of America. These symbols are reminders of what it is to be an American. Each place tells part of the story. So we need to embrace the relevance of our work. We have much to contribute—to individuals, to society, and even to ourselves—now more than ever.

To individuals who are attracted to our programs, we offer an engaging activity that is both recreational and educational. At the most basic level the program may be a diversion for someone—an antidote to despair. But there is much more.

At historic sites the program may offer a chance to better understand our history and to reflect on such universal concepts as liberty and justice. Many of our cultural sites celebrate the drama of human conduct. The story of our nation includes many men and women who have exhibited great courage and integrity in the face of adversity. What of our past helps us to better understand the present? What are we called to do, as individuals, in light of our past? Answers can be found as interpreters make meaning of events and help individuals personalize those meanings.

Similarly, a natural history program offers the opportunity to connect with the beauty found in nature. It may offer moments for contemplation and reflection. We can celebrate the stability, predictability, and resilience of nature. Rachel Carson wrote:

> There is a symbolic as well as actual beauty in the migration of birds.... There is something infinitely healing in the repeated refrains of nature—the assurance that dawn comes after night, and spring after winter.

The beauty of nature and a greater understanding of its wonders can comfort and inspire us—especially in difficult times. Individuals can find solace and direction through interpretation, now more than ever.

Identification with our land and culture helps to sustain us as a society. In Interpretation for the 21st Century we wrote, "Pride in our country—an understanding of our past, a concern for the present, and a vision for our future—stems from a close attachment to the land and our cultural roots." Historian Roderick Nash indicated that the landscape shaped our national character—one of independence, freedom, perseverance, and tenacity.

Furthermore, democracy requires an informed public and interpreters are a source of knowledge and inspiration in this regard. Thomas Jefferson wrote:

> I know of no safe depository of the ultimate powers of the society but the people themselves, and if we think them not enlightened enough to exercise that control with a wholesome discretion, the remedy is not to take it from them, but to inform their discretion.

As interpreters, we help to inform the discretion of those in our audiences. Through interpretation we enhance understanding and appreciation of our cultural and natural legacy—that which defines us as a democracy. Society has much to gain from our interpretive efforts, now more than ever.

The present circumstances provide each of us, as interpreters, an opportunity to give more of ourselves and through giving we receive blessings in return. Our love for America's culture and landscape allows us to provide this inspirational enjoyment to others.

We have daily opportunities to impact lives. We live in a country of proud history, diverse culture, and spectacular landscape. Our privilege—and obligation—is to help others to enjoy it, reflect upon it, and find meaning in it.

Our commitment to the profession of interpretation will enhance our own sense of purpose and well being. Our profession is a noble one, now more than ever.

A very real concern for many interpreters is the increased risk of working at some interpretive sites. Terrorists attacked symbols of the American way of life, and interpreters are defined as working at those places that symbolize America's natural beauty and cultural history. Undoubtedly, there will be increased security at places such as Independence National Historic Park, the Statue of Liberty, the Washington Monument, as well as dam sites such as Hoover, Glen Canyon, and Grand Coulee. Interpreters, like firefighters, are a profession and a family. It is our fervent hope and prayer that all our members remain safe.

We need to be connected and support each other in a reaffirmation of civilized values—now more than ever.

The Meaning of Interpretation: The Gift of Hope

The full original article appeared in the Journal of Interpretation Research. *It has been used, recently, in a training venue for the NASA-NPS Earth to Sky Project in which NASA scientists are working with NPS interpreters on cutting edge work related to the interpretation of global climate change. This essay also served as the initial inspiration for the conclusion of* Interpretation for the 21st Century *in which we explore our notion that interpretation is a gift.*

Part of the attraction of interpretation is its mystery. There is something unfathomable about it. Like religion, there is paradox, but that only lends itself to the power inherent in interpretation. If you could clarify it precisely, it would lose some of its power. To those practicing interpretation as a profession there is always an ideal out there, just out of reach. As Freeman Tilden pointed out, we are humbled because we fall short, in our own judgment, of the "flying perfect" at which we aim.

According to Enos Mills and Freeman Tilden, interpretation is an art form. Like any art, meaningful interpretation takes time. It is a creative act, bringing together disparate parts to make a whole. It is highly individualistic. Each interpreter's product will be different—personalized by one's background, experience, knowledge, imagination, creativity, and tenacity. The interpreter is taking the elements of a landscape or events from history, and relating them to broader meanings through his or her own experience.

An interpretive experience is among the art forms that can transform us. It can be in the company of theater or a life-changing book. But that same dramatic performance or piece of literature may not have a similar impact on everyone. We each read books and observe theater as no one else does. Likewise, the response to interpretation is deeply personal and individualistic.

Effective interpretation is successful in creating opportunities for people to form their own intellectual and emotional connections to the meanings and significance associated with a place. Moreover, many people respond entirely to the inspirational powers of nature without the assistance of outside interpretation—indeed, they may create their own inspired works, their own expressions of creative response. So, interpretation is personal both in its development and in its reception.

We have argued that interpretation is needed now more than ever. At historic sites, interpretive programs offer opportunities to better understand our history and to reflect on such universal concepts as liberty, justice, and civic responsibility. Many of our cultural sites celebrate the drama of human conduct—men and women who have exhibited great courage and integrity in the face of adversity. Natural history programs offer opportunities to connect with the beauty of the landscape—the stability, predictability, and resilience of nature. The splendor of the environment and a greater understanding of its wonders can comfort and inspire us. Through interpretation we enhance understanding and appreciation of our cultural and natural legacy—that which defines us as a democracy. We help others to see the meanings carried within a landscape or an event in history, and in that regard our work is a gift to our audiences.

Lewis Hyde described a work of art as a gift. If interpretation is an art (as Mills and Tilden expressed), and a work of art is a gift, then it follows that interpretation is a gift. The interpreter, like the artist, bears a gift that may have multiple meanings and can transform lives. As we stated in Interpretation for the 21st Century, "In the presence of meaningful art, we feel as if we have been touched by a resonating chord. At its absolute best, this is what all art, including interpretation, is about."

Inspired interpretation will offer a multitude of gifts depending on the recipients' needs, desires, and ability and willingness to accept the gift. As in any gift-giving, the giver wishes to please those receiving the gifts. Therefore, we must know something about those we interpret to. The best gift is one that offers something personal based on an understanding of the recipient.

To some people, interpreters provide the gift of knowledge, to others the gift of community, to others the gift of epiphany. Interpreters set the stage for great memories. Interpreters can provide the backdrop for an optimal experience so deep it cannot be fully described—when one feels a sense of exhilaration, a greater joy in living, a better understanding of one's place in the overall scheme, a positive hope for the future. We offer gifts of compassion and caring. We share the gift of love—for the landscape and the human condition.

Most of all, we believe, interpreters give the gift of hope. Our world is a place of incredible beauty and great joy, but also a place of environmental degradation and tremendous human suffering. We live amidst acts of cowardly terrorism and heroic compassion. If we are mired in fear, helplessness, or pessimism, then we are immobilized. Hope is indispensable.

Scott Russell Sanders wrote in Hunting for Hope:

> As we transform our own lives, we join with others who are making a kindred effort, and thus our work will be multiplied a thousandfold across the country and a millionfold around the earth. Whether all such efforts, added together, will be enough to avert disaster and bring about a just and enduring way of life, no one can say. In order to live in hope we needn't believe that everything will turn out well. We need only believe that we are on the right path.

To give hope, interpreters themselves must possess hope. Interpreters without hope in the future would offer a hollow message. They would lack the motivation and passion that comes from believing people have the power to change things for the better.

Hope is indeed indispensable. The greatest risk to both individuals and society is loss of hope for the future. A loss of hope that we can improve our personal lives, our communities, and our world leads to apathy, anger, or despair. Interpreters can offer hope to individuals for a rich, fulfilled life and hope in a future whereby generations to come inherit a prosperous and beautiful world. The beauty of human integrity commemorated in events of the past and the beauty of the intricacies of nature give rise to hope, and these are the tools of the interpreter.

So interpretation is a process of profound gift-giving. This process has many nuances and lacks precise definition, but that is the mystery of interpretation. In our estimation, it is fitting that a precise definition of interpretation is just beyond reach. Indeed, it is probably better that way. For gift-giving should not be directed by definition, but should come from a conviction of the heart.

Conclusion: A Profession of Hope

This essay explores the true meaning of hope and illustrates that hope is an essential ingredient for effective and passionate interpretation. As with the previous essay, portions of this essay will appear in the conclusion of Interpretation for the 21st Century *(third edition).*

Hope allows us to be happy and productive in spite of circumstances. Vaclav Havel, while imprisoned, wrote these words, "Hope is an orientation of the spirit. It transcends the world that is immediately experienced, and is anchored somewhere beyond the horizons."

Admiral Jim Stockdale, a prisoner of war during the Vietnam War, sheds more light on the difference between optimism and a deeper faith in a brighter future. Admiral Stockdale, the highest-ranking officer in the Hanoi Hilton, was tortured more than 20 times over eight years and even beat himself with a stool and cut himself with a razor so that he could not be used in propaganda films as a "well-treated prisoner." In his book, Good to Great, author Jim Collins relates a conversation with Admiral Stockdale wherein the admiral tells how he survived and why others didn't: "I never lost faith in the end of the story. I never doubted that not only I would get out, but also that I would prevail in the end and turn the experience into the defining event of my life, which, in retrospect, I would not trade."

That fact that Stockdale had hope in how the story would end is both amazing and encouraging. However, it is when he spoke about who did not make it that we can especially learn an important lesson about hope. When asked about who did not survive, he said, "Oh that's easy, the optimists." These were the prisoners who thought they'd be out by Christmas. And when Christmas passed they thought they'd be out by Easter. And when Easter passed they thought they would be out by Thanksgiving. And then they were back at Christmas again. Stockdale said, these optimists "died of a broken heart."

The lesson that Stockdale shared with Jim Collins is "to never confuse faith that you will prevail in the end—which you can never afford to lose—with the discipline to confront the most brutal facts of your current reality, whatever they might be." This then is the difference between naïve optimism and hope. Interpreters can offer hopeful messages, while acknowledging and confronting the many problems that shape our world.

Hope is critical to conservation efforts. Some African conservationists believe that it is too late to teach children to protect nature because by the time the children have the ability to set policies to preserve their patrimony, nothing will be left. They have lost hope. Some Western conservationists, overcome by disappointment and discouraged, have left Africa and returned home in defeat. They too have lost hope. Regarding conservation in Africa, Lester Brown said, "The greatest risk in Africa is the loss of hope." Loss of hope is a risk to conservation in developed countries too as conservationists become discouraged by the apathy or antagonism of their fellow citizens and a lack of support from policy-makers and regulators. Hopeful people are willing to work on long-term endeavors such as nature conservation, in spite of obstacles.

Hope is also fundamental to personal well-being. Hygiene, health, and social skills can be linked to hope. According to psychologist Paul Quinnett, research shows that people who scored high on a "hope scale" had shorter recovery times from surgeries, and lower incidences of premature death, heart disease, cancer, accidental death, and suicide. In fact, scores on the hope scale are the single best predictor of suicidal tendencies. Hopeful people are more extroverted and try harder at their jobs. Hopeful people brushed and flossed their teeth more often. When people have no hope they no longer care about the future of their world or themselves. Hopeless people are immobilized by apathy or fear. Hopeful people are healthier, more social, and more productive.

If there is general agreement that unsocial and uncaring individuals cannot be effective interpreters, then it follows that interpreters must have hope. To offer hope, interpreters must possess that "orientation of the spirit" and a sense of something "beyond the horizon" that feeds their dedication and passion. If interpreters are hope-less, if they believe the world is on a dark path to destruction and suffering, and if they feel powerless to affect change, they become nothing more than prophets of doom, spreading fear, apathy, or dread instead of enriching lives. What would be the point of devoting a career to interpretation if one had no hope for a better future? Without hope there would be no purpose, and without purpose there would be no passion, and without passion interpretation is hollow and weak. If by definition interpreters are enthusiastic provokers of action and thought, then in a sense, a hope-less interpreter is an oxymoron.

Interpreters are well-placed to be purveyors of hope. As we noted in the previous essay, the repeated refrains of nature and the intricacies of nature give hope. Human creativity, integrity, and courage as demonstrated in historic events give hope. We have solved seemingly impossible challenges in the past. With educated understanding, focused effort, and integrity we can do it again.

In recognition of the power of nature to heal and give hope, the U.S. Congress asked the U.S. Forest Service to create a Living Memorials Project (LMP) to create lasting living memorials to the victims of 9/11 and their families and communities. Cost-share funds and technical support were provided to communities and individuals desiring to create such memorials. In addition to the trees and gardens themselves, interpretive plaques, signage, and brochures add meaning at many of these sites. The goal of the LMP was "to amplify community actions in the post-9/11 context and to connect these decentralized, yet common, threads of expression and hope." The Forest Service conducted an inventory and created a registry, which now includes more than 600 sites in all 50 states and several foreign countries, each an expression of hope.

On an even larger scale, the holocaust also provided for hope-filled interpretation. The Holocaust Museum does a masterful job of interjecting hope amidst the horror of the holocaust. On the final floor after completing the stunningly sad tour through the permanent exhibition, visitors are presented with exhibits about the liberation of the Nazi camps and the Allied victory over Nazi Germany, and heroic rescue and resistance efforts. Visitors, most now emotionally drained and dazed by the powerful experience, can view the film "Testimony," which introduces visitors to survivors, rescuers, and liberators who share their inspiring experiences. Guests leave with a sense of hope as they hear and see strong survivors, courageous non-Jewish neighbors who risked death or imprisonment to help people escape the Nazis, and postwar efforts to render justice to those who were guilty of these atrocities. Interpretation that focuses on hope in human nature include stories of French villagers in Le Chamon-sur-Lignon who hid Jews, the Danish rescue of 7,000 Jews, and Raoul Wallenberg's activities to save Jews in occupied Europe.

The most important thing interpreters can do, from developing countries to struggling communities, is to give hope through dynamic, hopeful messages and by demonstrating a hopeful lifestyle. G.K. Chesterton wrote, "As long as matters are really hopeful, hope is a mere flattery or platitude; it is only when everything is hopeless that hope begins to be a strength. Like all Christian virtues, it is as unreasonable as it is indispensable."

If thou indeed derive thy light from Heaven,
Then, to the measure of that heaven-born light,
Shine, Poet! in thy place, and be content: —
The stars pre-eminent in magnitude,
And they that from the zenith dart their beams,
(Visible though they be to half the earth,
Though half a sphere be conscious of their brightness)
Are yet of no diviner origin,
No purer essence, than the one that burns,
Like an untended watch-fire on the ridge
Of some dark mountain; or than those which seem
Humbly to hang, like twinkling winter lamps,
Among the branches of the leafless trees.
All are the undying offspring of one Sire:
Then, to the measure of the light vouchsafed,
Shine, Poet! in thy place, and be content.

— William Wordsworth

Original Sources

Voices from Literature and the Arts

Cable, T. (1992). To Enjoy Understandingly. Legacy, 3(2):8–9.

Beck, L. (1989). Conversations with Barry Lopez: Musings on Interpretation. Journal of Interpretation, 13(3):4–7.

Beck, L. (1989). Lee Stetson on Interpretation. Journal of Interpretation, 13(6):8-9.

Professionalism

Beck, L. and Cable, T. (1995). Resolving the Interpreter's Identity Problem. Legacy, 6(5):28–29.

Cable, T. (1999). Becoming Better Interpreters. Legacy, 10(6):14–16.

Application

Beck, L. (2006). A Pocketchange History of the Lewis and Clark Expedition and Environmental Consciousness in America. The Interpreter, 2(5):16–17.

Beck, L. (2006). Interpreting Our State's Heritage. The Interpreter, 2(6):18–19.

Universal Concepts

Beck, L. (2001). What is the Essence of Our Professional Responsibility? Legacy, 12(4):29–32.

Beck, L. (2005). Wicked Interpretation: Lessons from Broadway. The Interpreter, 1(4):14–17.

Global Interpretation

Cable, T. (2006). The Role of Interpretation in International Tourism. pp 71-77. Chapter in T. Merriman and L. Brochu eds, The History of Interpretation in the United States. InterpPress.

Beck, L. (2008). VolunTourism: Seeing the World and Saving the World. Legacy, 19(1):28–29.

Inspiration

Cable, T. (2003). Interpretive Lighthouses. Visions [NAI Region VI Newsletter] 16(4):1.

Cable, T. and Beck, L. (2001). The Need for Interpretation: Now More than Ever. Legacy, 12(5): 47.

Beck, L. and Cable, T. (2003). The Meaning of Interpretation. Journal of Interpretation Research, 7(1):7–10.

Acknowledgments

Ted Cable would like to thank his friends LuAnn Cadden, Robin Grumm, and Kevin Lohraff for inspiring and improving many of the essays that found their way into this book. Similarly, Larry Beck would like to thank Dan Dustin and Andrea Beck.

About the Authors

Larry Beck is a professor of recreation and tourism management at San Diego State University. He has a B.S. in natural resource planning and interpretation from Humboldt State University, M.A. in education from Azusa Pacific University, and Ph.D. in education from the University of Minnesota. Dr. Beck is the author/coauthor of four books and more than 100 articles on natural resource management, cultural and environmental interpretation, and higher education. He has received numerous awards for his teaching and scholarship, including the Meritorious Service Award from the National Association for Interpretation. He is a Faculty Fellow of People, Information, and Communication Technologies and a University Scholar of Universal Design for Learning.

Ted Cable is a professor of park management and conservation at Kansas State University. He has a B.S. in biology from the University of Illinois-Chicago, and both a M.S. in wildlife ecology and Ph.D. in forest recreation from Purdue University. Dr. Cable is the author/coauthor of 10 books and more than 150 articles on natural resource management, wildlife, and interpretation. He has consulted on conservation projects in more than 25 states, has designed several nature parks and preserves, and has worked on conservation projects in Latin America and Africa. In addition to having received numerous university awards, he is a Fellow of the National Association for Interpretation and has been honored by both the U.S. Environmental Protection Agency and the U.S. Department of Agriculture for outstanding teaching in the field of conservation and interpretation.